The COOP cookbook

■ ■ ■ ■ ■

The COOP cookbook

Delicious and Healthy Meals in Less Than Half an Hour

Rosemary Fifield

Illustrations by Robin Wimbiscus

CHELSEA GREEN PUBLISHING COMPANY

WHITE RIVER JUNCTION, VERMONT

TOTNES, ENGLAND

This book is dedicated with love
to my parents, who instilled in me their devotion
to vegetable gardening, whole foods cooking, and
sharing the bounty with family and friends.

© 2000 Rosemary Fifield.
Illustrations © 1996, 2000 Robin Wimbiscus.

Designed by Jill Shaffer.

Printed in the United States.
First printing, month year.

03 02 01 00   1 2 3 4 5

Library of Congress Cataloging-in-Publication Data

Fifield, Rosemary, 1945-
       The co-op cookbook : delicious and healthy meals in less than
half an hour / Rosemary Fifield.
              p.   cm.
       Includes index.
       ISBN 1-890132-47-0 (alk. paper)
       1. Quick and easy cookery.   I. Title.

       TX833.5 .F54 2000
       641.5'55—dc21   99-051597

Green Books Ltd
Foxhole, Dartington
Totnes, Devon TQ9 6EB, United Kingdom
44-1-803-863-843

Chelsea Green Publishing Company
Post Office Box 428
White River Junction, VT 05001
(800) 639-4099
www.chelseagreen.com

Contents

Hot Dishes 67

cold Salads 137

Index 153

Preface

THE HANOVER CO-OP'S "What's for Supper?" program began in October 1994, when I was working as the Co-op's food and nutrition educator. During the previous year, many food store customers and participants in the Co-op's popular cooking classes had expressed a wish for someone who would help them decide what to make for dinner on a busy day. Their needs were straightforward: They wanted tasty, healthful meals that were quick, easy, and economical, and that would appeal to the entire family.

Drawing on my own interest in cooking healthful meals from scratch, as well as on personal experience as a working wife and mother, I considered how best to share some of my personal favorites: one-dish meals based on fresh produce, legumes, pasta, rice, or other grains, and, occasionally, meat or seafood. I wanted to reinforce the idea that it is possible to make a meal in a short amount of time without resorting to frozen entrees, boxed meals, or canned spaghetti sauce. While not a completely "from scratch" approach, "What's for Supper?" recipes encourage the use of fresh vegetables whenever possible, and include a variety of grains, beans, seafood, and sometimes meat. In all cases, they strive to provide a balanced, lowfat meal.

In the original program, we introduced a weekly recipe on Wednesdays, with a chance for customers to sample the finished dish. The intention was to offer the shopper a strictly educational presentation with no product tie-ins. As the originator of the recipe, the cook, and the person handing it to the customer, I was able to provide information to each person based on his or her interests. It was an opportunity to discuss nutrition topics, unfamiliar ingredients, product substitutions, cooking techniques, use of herbs and spices, and so on. When asked, "So what are you selling here?" I took great pleasure in being able to say, "I'm not selling anything. This is a 30-minute recipe for you to take home and cook for yourself."

"What's for Supper?" meals are low in saturated fat, high in flavor, and can be ready to eat in approximately 30 minutes. They are designed to encourage the cook's creativity through the use of seasonal ingredient substitutions and the opportunity for variation of favorite grains, legumes, and other sources of complex carbohydrates. In addition, they combine familiar flavors and foods that family members of all ages will eat, while introducing new ways of preparing them to keep meals fresh and interesting.

The continued popularity of the "What's for Supper?" program indicates that it meets our shoppers' need for healthful, quick, and easy meals with wide-ranging appeal. With this in mind, I have compiled one hundred of my favorite recipes.

Rosemary Fifield
Education Director
Hanover Consumer Cooperative Society, Inc.
Hanover, New Hampshire

■　■　■

Acknowledgments

MY APPRECIATION of whole fresh foods began in the gardens of my Sicilian-born grandfather, Gaetano Balistrieri, who devoted his entire urban backyard to food production. Growing up in the house next door, I often visited his extensive vegetable garden, which was overhung by a large pear tree and bordered by a grape arbor and a chicken coop full of hens (an illegal carry-over from the days of World War II). In that garden, he grew everything from tomatoes to kohlrabi, and I learned, early on, the joys of eating directly from the source.

My parents, Patricia and Edward Balistrieri, were also dedicated gardeners, providing the fragile raspberries that adorned my breakfast cereal, as well as the crispy cucumbers they transformed into dozens of jars of dill pickles each year. Eating seasonally was the norm in those days of iceberg lettuce and tasteless hothouse tomatoes, and my mother's sweet-and-sour cabbage is still a personal winter favorite. My parents shared the cooking, and I learned through their example, rather than through the use of recipes.

Growing and cooking whole foods is only part of the total enjoyment; one needs an appreciative audience. My husband, Don Fifield, and my son, Nick Yager, have ably filled that role, and many of the recipes in this book are variations on their favorites.

The introduction and success of the "What's for Supper?" program at the Hanover Co-op could not have occurred without the encouragement and enthusiasm of former Education Director Kate Read. I will always appreciate her faith in me and her willingness to let me run with my ideas. I would also like to thank Gail Haubrich, former manager of

Acknowledgments
■ ■ ■ ■ ■

the Hanover Co-op Prepared Foods Kitchen, whose dedication to the production of wholesome, nutritious food is an inspiration.

I am grateful to Chelsea Green Publisher Stephen Morris and Editor-in-Chief Jim Schley for their interest in this project, and to my editor, Rachael Cohen, for her insightful suggestions.

And last, but never least, I wish to thank the members and customers of the Co-op Food Stores in Hanover and Lebanon, New Hampshire, and of co-ops around the world for their farsighted support of a better way of doing business—the consumer cooperative.

The
COOP
cookbook

OVER ONE HUNDRED FIFTY YEARS OF

Successful cooperation

T HE FIRST SUCCESSFUL CONSUMER COOPERATIVE, operating on the democratic principle of "one member, one vote," was organized in 1844 by twenty-eight working people in the town of Rochdale, England. Calling themselves the Rochdale Equitable Pioneers Society, they sought to achieve both economic and social justice. One hundred fifty years later, the movement they started boasts over 720 million members worldwide.

The Rochdale Pioneers were weavers who organized in an effort to control not only the cost of their food, but its purity as well. At a time

ROCHDALE MUSEUM

Fourteen of the original twenty-eight Rochdale Pioneers, who founded the first cooperative in 1844. The Pioneers were handloom weavers and other working people seeking wholesome food for their families.

when a pound of pure tea cost a day's wage, poor working people were forced to purchase adulterated food. Sugar contained pounded rice, and pepper was stretched with pounded nut shells. Flour commonly included plaster or ground bones, while leaves and iron filings were mixed with tea. Food adulteration was so common that when pure flour and other products were made available to people through the first Rochdale store, customers complained about their taste. Dishonest shopkeepers added to the insult by using false weights and measures to their advantage.

Basing their business on "pure food" and "honest weight," the Pioneers opened their first little store four days before Christmas of 1844. Their inventory consisted of butter, sugar, flour, oatmeal, and tallow candles. The candles were an afterthought, the result of the gas company's refusal to supply the shop with gas for its lights. The new shop owners purchased candles in bulk and sold the extras to shoppers. Following on their commitment to community, they established cooperative housing, a co-op bank, and producer cooperatives by the 1870s.

The Rochdale Pioneers Museum is sited in the original cooperative food store at No. 31 Toad Lane, Rochdale, England.

While the Rochdale Pioneers were not the first individuals to work together cooperatively, they were responsible for the principles that guide cooperatives today. "One member, one vote"—in contrast to voting by shares of stock—was a revolutionary idea. They built capital by collecting weekly subscriptions from members. Patronage was rewarded with a return from profits proportional to purchases made during the year, a concept that continues to distinguish cooperatives from other types of business. The emphasis on pure, wholesome food remains an objective of consumer co-ops to this day.

Education was also of utmost importance to the Society and continues to be an integral part of cooperatives. The Pioneers recognized that knowledge is power and sought to educate their members through lectures, discussions, and development of a heretofore unknown free library on the second floor of their store. They established an education committee, and as the Rochdale cooperative flourished and began to open more stores, each was designed to include a library and reading room.

Today, cooperatives of all types abound around the world, including cooperatives for farmers and other producers, independent grocers, wholesalers, small businesses, and large businesses. Cooperatives have been created to provide for child care, housing, banking, energy, and other services as well as for products. The International Cooperative Alliance, established in 1895, now includes over one hundred member countries. In the Basque Region of Spain, the Mondragon system of cooperatives serves over twenty-five thousand worker-owners who benefit from an educational institute, a bank, housing, and over one hundred independent worker-owned enterprises as well as an enterprise division.

Cooperation helps small business owners compete with large businesses through increased purchasing power for everything from supplies to insurance to marketing. And it continues to benefit individuals who wish to acquire goods and services not readily available in their area. Canadian cooperatives ensure that people in remote areas of the country have access to the goods they need. In 1938, a group of mountaineers in Seattle, Washington, wanted to import quality climbing gear from Europe. They formed Recreational Equipment, which has become the largest consumer cooperative in the United States today, serving over 1.3 million members.

During the Great Depression, U.S. consumers established a number of food cooperatives across the country in an effort to provide themselves

THE *Cooperative Principles* AND *Statement* OF *Cooperative Identity*

The International Cooperative Alliance, established in 1895, is considered to be the final authority for defining cooperatives and the principles by which they operate. The organization has made three formal statements of cooperative principles over the past one hundred years in an effort to keep them relevant to the contemporary world. At its one hundredth anniversary meeting in September 1995 in Manchester, England, the Alliance adopted the following "Statement of Cooperative Identity."

DEFINITION

A cooperative is an autonomous association of persons united voluntarily to meet their common economic, social, and cultural needs and aspirations through a jointly owned and democratically controlled enterprise.

VALUES

Cooperatives are based on the values of self-help, self-responsibility, democracy, equality, equity, and solidarity. In the tradition of their founders, cooperative members believe in the ethical values of honesty, openness, social responsibility, and caring for others.

PRINCIPLES

The cooperative principles are guidelines by which cooperatives put their values into practice.

1. *Voluntary and Open Membership.* Cooperatives are voluntary organizations, open to all persons able to use their services and willing to accept the responsibilities of membership, without gender, social, racial, political, or religious discrimination.

2. *Democratic Member Control.* Cooperatives are democratic organizations controlled by their members, who actively participate in setting their policies and making decisions. Men and women serv-

ing as elected representatives are accountable to the membership. In primary cooperatives, members have equal voting rights (one member, one vote), and cooperatives at other levels are also organized in a democratic manner.

3. *Member Economic Participation.* Members contribute equitably to, and democratically control, the capital of their cooperative. At least part of that capital is usually the common property of the cooperative. Members usually receive limited compensation, if any, on capital subscribed as a condition of membership. Members allocate surpluses for any of the following purposes: developing their cooperative, possibly by setting up reserves, part of which at least would be indivisible; benefiting members in proportion to their transactions with the cooperative; and supporting other activities approved by the membership.

4. *Autonomy and Independence.* Cooperatives are autonomous, self-help organizations controlled by their members. If they enter into agreements with other organizations, including governments, or raise capital from external sources, they do so on terms that ensure democratic control by their members and maintain their cooperative autonomy.

5. *Education, Training, and Information.* Cooperatives provide education and training for their members, elected representatives, managers, and employees so they can contribute effectively to the development of their cooperatives. They inform the general public—particularly young people and opinion leaders—about the nature and benefits of cooperation.

6. *Cooperation Among Cooperatives.* Cooperatives serve their members most effectively and strengthen the cooperative movement by working together through local, national, regional, and international structures.

7. *Concern for Community.* Cooperatives work for the sustainable development of their communities, through policies approved by their members.

SOURCE: *The International Cooperative Alliance, 1995.*

with quality products at an affordable price. The 1970s saw a second wave of new food cooperatives as health-conscious consumers once again sought to achieve control over the purity of the food they purchased. Many of these cooperatives began as neighborhood buying clubs, where families came together to purchase bulk goods in quantity. Members shared the task of dividing up the food into smaller units and sorting it for pickup. In time, the more successful clubs opened storefronts, and the cooperative natural food store was born.

Today, over three hundred consumer cooperatives operate food stores in the United States, some with more than one location. Eight cooperative distributors, each serving a multistate area, supply retail stores and buying clubs with natural foods. National and regional support organizations, such as the University of Wisconsin Center for Cooperatives, the National Cooperative Business Association, and the National Cooperative Bank, serve as resources for information on cooperatives, financial support, marketing expertise, and other needs.

In addition to supplying their members and customers with quality food products, food cooperatives also strive to provide them with trustworthy information about those products. Like the Rochdale Equitable Pioneers Society, today's co-ops emphasize the health and well-being of their members and their community as well as fair prices, good customer service, and top quality merchandise.

The Hanover Consumer Cooperative Society

The Hanover Consumer Cooperative Society was also born of economic need and a desire for better quality food during difficult economic times. A child of the Great Depression, the Hanover Co-op began when a group of neighbors—mostly Dartmouth College professors and their wives—gathered in December of 1935 to discuss ways to bring high quality food to Hanover at better prices.

Hanover, New Hampshire, is a small college town located on the banks of the Connecticut River, roughly two hours north of Boston.

Dominated by Dartmouth College, Hanover is picturesque, gentrified, and isolated. Its Main Street is approximately three blocks long and consists of small shops and independently owned restaurants. The closest cities of any size are Concord and Manchester, New Hampshire and Burlington, Vermont, each at least one hour away.

The major employers in Hanover have always been Dartmouth College, Dartmouth Medical School, and, until its move in September 1991, Mary Hitchcock Memorial Hospital and the Hitchcock Clinic. In the mid-1930s, Dartmouth faculty were struggling with the effects of a 10 percent wage decrease while faced with the usual limited resources for perishable foods. As one founding member describes it, "We used to buy rotten fruit from a chain store on Main Street. And they'd be in a bag—say, six grapefruits—and you'd come home and find two rotten. So you'd go back and the very nice produce man would say, 'Well, I'll replace them, but it comes out of my own pocket.' That made us mad."

On January 6, 1936, about thirty members of the community met for the purpose of organizing a buying club. They voted to organize a local cooperative buyers group to be called "The Hanover Consumers Club." Seventeen families signed on as charter members and paid the one dollar fee.

They began by ordering bushel baskets of oranges and grapefruit directly from Florida. The citrus was stored in one member's garage, where all would come to pick up their orders. In time, the group added local butter and milk, canned fruits and vegetables, dried fruit, potatoes, and maple syrup. The Club also arranged with local suppliers for discounts on gasoline, fuel oil, and coal.

At meetings, members shared information on other types of goods and services, including locally made German sausage and pumpernickel bread, table wines, and silk hosiery as well as house painting, skate sharpening, oil burners, and men's tailor-made suits. The ladies held tasting parties to compare various brands of canned fruit to determine which had the most fruit and which had the most water. Two informational bulletins per week were edited, mimeographed, and delivered by bicycle to all members, one dealing with the history and principles of cooperative societies, the other giving information about good buys from various sources of supply.

With the addition of Co-op label canned goods from a co-op whole-saler in New York, the distribution point was moved to a member's basement. Shelves were built along one wall, and members came and went through the bulkhead. By November 1936, members felt that the Hanover Consumers Club should be transformed into a larger and more formal organization. They voted to incorporate as the Hanover Con-sumer Cooperative Society, accepting articles of agreement and bylaws for the new entity and issuing their first stock certificates. At the December meeting, they agreed to rent the basement of a barbershop on Main Street to house their new store.

The first consumer cooperative store in New Hampshire opened in January 1937. By March 3, it had 124 members, representing 96 fami-lies. Roger Bristol, a founding member, resigned his position as a teacher at Hanover High School to become the manager and sole employee. Sales for the first year topped $11,000. In 1938, the store moved to larger quarters in the basement of a building across the street, and at the end of that year showed sufficient profit to pay a patronage refund of 3 percent to its members.

By the end of 1939, annual sales had risen to over $29,300 and membership stood at 318. Membership and gross sales continued to grow throughout 1940, making it increasingly difficult to provide ser-vices in the cramped quarters below street level. When the restaurant above the Co-op went out of business in 1941, the members considered the rather heady thought of leasing the newly available first floor space in addition to the basement.

To do so, the cooperative needed to raise capital for new furnish-ings, the salary for a full-time assistant, and other incidental expenses. Members were asked to buy more shares, but it was wartime, and all were financially strapped and limited in what they could do. Borrowing

The Co-op staff in 1963, take just before the grand opening of the Co-op at its new Park Street site. FRONT ROW (LEFT TO RIGHT): *Agnes Gilbody, Lorraine Mousley, Alice Hawes, Evelyn Mayette, Lillian Wing, Marion Williams.* MIDDLE ROW: *Melvin Coburn, Nelson Potwin, Ernest Fontaine, Maurice LaCroix, Ulrich Holzinger.* BACK ROW: *Gary Clay, Philip Coburn, Bayard Mousley, Maurice Crate, Max Mousley.*

from the local bank was out of the question—the president of the bank was reputed to have said that the co-op was "communist infiltration into a respectable town." Still, without an additional $1,600, the Co-op would have to postpone the move or look for another basement.

The late Arthur Jensen, president of the Co-op board in 1941, describes how he solved the dilemma on the Co-op's history video called *Hand In Hand*:

> I was sitting there one afternoon with [the treasurer and the store manager] when down the stairs to make a purchase came Professor Gerould of the Chemistry Department. I didn't know him well, but I knew him, so as a sort of greeting

■ ■ ■

9

I said, 'Professor Gerould, you couldn't by chance loan us $1,600 for six months, could you?' Professor Gerould stopped in the middle of the store, was silent for a minute, pursed his lips, and then said, 'I guess I could.' So I said, 'Let's go across the street to the bank.' We went to the bank, transferred $1,600 from his account to the Co-op account, and then went back and he bought his groceries. [Arthur smiles at this point.] I should have asked for $2,000.

The Co-op opened its doors above ground for the first time in the summer of 1942 and became the first self-service food store in Hanover. The United States was at war, which meant rationing and shortages, and

The Co-op Principles and the Twin Pines cooperative symbol made their Hanover debut in 1961, when the Co-op celebrated its 25th anniversary with a parade down Main Street.

with each passing day Co-op shelves became more empty. Throughout World War II, business committee members voluntarily worked in the store unloading trucks, opening cartons, and stocking shelves. By the end of the 1940s, however, the Co-op was in deep financial difficulty. Several other food stores occupied Main Street, and to compete, the Co-op needed to add frozen foods, fresh meat, and a wider selection of fruits and vegetables. But it had neither the capital nor the space to achieve this. The Co-op desperately required the firm hand of a good manager if it was to survive, let alone succeed.

Arthur Jensen came to the rescue once more. In his travels, he encountered an impressive manager at a small food co-op in Massachusetts. Using all of his powers of persuasion, he convinced Harry Gerstenberger to move to Hanover to manage the Co-op Food Store. Harry arrived in 1949 to find a very small store with very limited selection. There were no coolers for the produce, and the only meats were pre-packaged items such as bacon. The store lacked a loading dock, storage space, office space, and parking. To make matters worse, the previous manager had amassed a large inventory of slow-moving items, badly compromising the Co-op's cash flow and storage space.

"I think it was bringing in Gerstenberger that saved the Co-op," Arthur Jensen says in the video. "He gave his whole life to the organization . . . he knew how to handle people, how to manage." Nan King, another founding member, describes Harry Gerstenberger as "a real cooperator who loved people, and he loved to be an educator. He was in the store talking with people a lot of the time and knew the members very well. . . . We treasured Harry Gerstenberger."

The Co-op thrived under Harry's management, and by 1958, when space became available in the remainder of the building, the store had the capital to double in size. By 1962, Co-op membership reached two thousand with $1 million per year in sales. But, the Co-op still had no parking lot. Employees from that time period remember carrying groceries from one end of Main Street to the other, and it became obvious to management that a grocery store in the middle of downtown was impractical.

■ ■ ■

Growth and Future Planning

The Co-op's board began to look at sites on the edge of town. At several large, contentious meetings, members debated the need for growth and future planning. Many members feared the consequences of leaving the Main Street location and predicted that people would not travel to buy groceries on the outskirts of Hanover. Still, the membership voted to purchase land on the southern edge of town, and, in 1963, the Co-op built a new store on the site it occupies today.

Harry Gerstenberger retired in 1965, and his nephew, Arthur Gerstenberger, who had worked beside him at the Hanover Co-op since 1949, took over as general manager. Under Arthur, the Co-op continued to grow, expanding its services to its members and community. In 1985, the Co-op purchased the service station that adjoined its property and added gasoline and car repair to the services available to members. Arthur presided over the fiftieth anniversary celebration of the Hanover Consumer Cooperative Society in 1986 as well as the first expansion of the food store at its current site in the same year. As beloved by Co-op members as his uncle before him, Arthur Gerstenberger retired in December 1988.

The current general manager, Terry Appleby, a veteran of Puget Consumer Cooperative in Seattle, Washington, was hired in 1992. At that time, the Co-op's annual sales from the food store and the service center were $17.6 million. In 1994, with an overcrowded store and a parking lot that could no longer accommodate the ever-increasing number of people shopping at the Co-op, a second expansion and remodeling of the Hanover store was done. The Co-op added a second Co-op service center on the north end of Hanover in December 1995.

As early as 1991, the board was considering the possibility of opening a second store, as membership and patronage at the Hanover location continued to increase. Crowding in the store and in the parking lot had begun to cause shoppers to go elsewhere, and the expansion and remodeling to be done in 1994 would prove to be only a stop-gap mea-

Co-op General Manager Harry Gerstenberger (LEFT) and Assistant Manager Arthur Gerstenberger survey the progress of the Co-op Food Store at its new Park Street location in 1963.

sure. Surveys, focus groups, and extra member meetings were conducted to gauge member reaction to the idea of a second location. While some opposed the concept of multiple stores, more were concerned that the opening of a second location would herald the end of the much beloved Hanover store. Some feared the financial burden of a second retail operation and worried that the membership could not support two Co-op stores.

The question of building a second store was brought to the membership for a vote at the Annual Meeting in April 1996. The site that had been chosen was two miles south of the Hanover store, in the adjoining town of Lebanon, New Hampshire. The property belonged to Dartmouth College, which was putting in a development to be known as Centerra. Among the projects planned for the area was a marketplace that would include a grocery store as its anchor, and the Co-op was

■ ■ ■

HANOVER CONSUMER CO-OP

Hanover Food Co-op board members formed the Precision Grocery Cart Drill Team in celebration of the store's fiftieth anniversary in 1986. The Hanover Co-op is one of the oldest food cooperatives in operation in the United States.

Dartmouth's first choice. After members spoke passionately both for and against the motion to open a second store on that site, the motion was voted on and passed.

Although Dartmouth owns the property, the Co-op actively participated in designing the new store. Both entities made a commitment to apply principles of environmentally conscious design, including energy conservation, daylighting with concurrent automatic dimming controls, advanced mechanical systems, advanced refrigeration systems, and recycled and environmentally benign materials. Construction materials with recycled content included the concrete floors (fly-ash), steel stud framing, wood timbers, fiberglass insulation, extruded polystyrene, vapor retarders, millwork, countertops, carpeting, resilient flooring, and some floor tiles.

■ ■ ■

New England Electric Systems participated in making the new Co-op a demonstration project, and through its incentive program, brought down the cost of some building improvements related to energy savings. Although achieving these savings in operational costs required additional initial investment on the part of the Co-op, the cost-benefit ratio is very favorable. Compared to a standardized store, energy conservation savings are projected to be in the range of $55,000 a year.

Health and safety issues for employees and shoppers were also addressed, including air quality, light quality, and thermal comfort. And, working from experience, Co-op planners were careful to include "adaptability to change" among the top priorities. Education of members and customers regarding the "green" aspects of the store's construction became an important goal, culminating in tours of the facility that point out the environmentally conscious aspects of the store's design.

The Lebanon Co-op Food Store at Centerra Marketplace opened its doors in October 1997. In addition to having an entirely different design from the Hanover store, it incorporated new ideas such as an extensive prepared foods kitchen and a sit-down café. In the first three months of operation, nearly 850 new memberships were added through the Lebanon store alone, with an additional 150 in Hanover. Over 1,600 new memberships were opened in 1998, the majority of them through the new Lebanon store, bringing total memberships in the Hanover Consumer Cooperative Society, to over 17,000, representing more than 24,000 individuals.

In 1998, the two Co-op stores, along with the service centers, grossed over $34.7 million, and patronage continues to grow. In May 1999, the Co-op converted its second service center into the Co-op Community Food Market. A convenience-type store, this newest Co-op endeavor brings the best of the Co-op to a neighborhood market, including fresh quality produce, natural foods, prepared foods from our kitchens, locally made baked goods, natural health and beauty aids, high quality wine, microbrewery beers, and Equal Exchange coffee. The

■ ■ ■

gas pumps make it a convenience store, but the prices remain the same as those in the food stores.

Many challenges lie ahead as the Hanover Consumer Cooperative Society approaches its sixty-fifth anniversary. Inspired by the success of natural food co-ops, mainstream grocers now carry many of the same products, including organically raised produce, natural foods, and supplements. Specialty food stores and chains abound. Modern transportation and purchasing over the Internet give shoppers access to anything and everything year-round. The Co-op's leaders must constantly ask themselves: What will distinguish the Co-op from its competition in the years to come?

PHTO © JOHN DOUGLAS/FLYING SQUIRREL

The Hanover Co-op's continued success led to the opening of a second food store in nearby Lebanon, New Hampshire, in 1997. The Lebanon Co-op building utilizes recycled materials and ecological principles such as daylighting to increase energy efficiency and improve employee comfort.

Among the answers is consumer education. A 1994 study done by the Gallup Poll, titled "Awareness and Image of Business Cooperatives: A Survey of the American Public," showed that two-thirds of Americans trust a cooperative more than an investor-owned business. Consumers trust cooperatives to give them truthful information about individual products, food production, packaging, nutrition, and other food-related issues. Just as the Rochdale Pioneers recognized that knowledge is power, today's food co-ops continue to empower their members and shoppers by keeping them abreast of the latest information.

Food co-ops also draw their strength from being grounded in the communities where they operate. Locally owned businesses have more stake in the welfare of their community, and a member-owned business is a powerful form of local ownership. Co-ops purchase locally and support local growers and producers. In rural settings like New Hampshire and Vermont, supporting local growers means helping to ensure the future of the family farm and the rural way of life. This, in turn, ensures that local food production will always exist should increased transportation costs someday threaten the food supply in remote areas such as northern New England.

Finally, being a member-owner of a consumer co-op gives a unique sense of belonging and community that other retail operations cannot provide. "Concern for community" is the seventh Cooperative Principle, and for many members, their co-op provides a means to make a social difference. Whether they actively volunteer to participate in co-op outreach activities, or simply support their co-op's philanthropic programs through their patronage, co-op members can take pride in the community efforts put forth in their name. Couple that with the sense of camaraderie that exists among shoppers and co-op staff, and you have a unique food-shopping experience that cannot be duplicated by a for-profit retailer.

This doesn't mean that food co-ops can become complacent; the management and board of the Hanover Consumer Cooperative Society are well aware of that. But through continuous quality improvement programs, over-the-top customer service, and diligent attention to member and customer needs, the Co-op should always be able to maintain its place as an important force that enriches the lives of area consumers.

Member and Consumer Education

Member and consumer education has played a major role in cooperatives since the days of the Rochdale Pioneers. Through speakers, courses, free libraries, and reading rooms, the Pioneers provided learning opportunities to their members and shoppers on a variety of social, economic, and consumer topics. Today, the importance of education, training, and information is maintained as the fifth Cooperative Principle.

Member education at the Hanover Consumers Club began upon the Club's inception with the publication of two weekly bulletins that covered cooperative and consumer issues, respectively. Tasting committees met to evaluate the quality of new products, such as Jell-O, while other members sought good bargains and shared the information with their fellows. The 1936 bylaws of the Club include the provision for a standing committee to be known as the "Education and Membership Committee, composed of three or more members, (which) shall strive toward the education of members and consumers at large in the significance of social and economic problems as they affect consumers as such, and in their role as producers."

The Hanover Co-op's first official education secretary was Sally Gerstenberger, wife of Harry Gerstenberger who was hired as general manager in 1949. Both Sally and Harry were dyed-in-the-wool cooperators, and although she was never a paid employee of the Co-op, Sally's efforts as a volunteer and her enthusiasm for cooperatives left a lasting legacy in the Co-op's commitment to providing consumer information and cooperative education. Prior to 1972, the Co-op had no paid education staff, and all educational programs were carried out by an active education committee. Together with other members, Sally produced the Co-op's monthly bulletin and bought space in the local newspaper to promote the Co-op message, educating readers about cooperative principles and benefits of member ownership. At one point, Sally plastered the front windows of the store with canceled refund checks to illustrate the money given back to the community.

The board hired its first on-staff education director in 1972. The purpose of the half-time position was "educating membership and public at large in matters of consumer concern, nutrition, environmental problems; encouraging members; promoting cooperative principles."

This was to be accomplished through the monthly bulletin, weekly specials sheets, advertising copy, educational demonstrations in-store, tracking consumer legislation on the state and national level, comparative shopping, monitoring and reporting on product quality, and educating the staff in co-op principles.

Over the years, the education department has expanded and today includes, in addition to the education director, a registered dietitian, a marketing director, a member and community outreach coordinator, a member services coordinator, a food programs coordinator, a graphic artist, and several personnel at the information desks in both stores. Consumer information, marketing, cooperative education, and membership issues are addressed by the staff through the bi-monthly Co-op News, in-store displays, an extensive selection of staff-generated brochures, sampling demos, cooking demonstrations, shelf tags, specials sheets, and personal interaction. The Co-op offers over sixty cooking classes and lectures to its members and shoppers each year as well as bringing nutrition and food preparation information to senior centers, employee wellness programs, health fairs, and private groups. With area nonprofit organizations, the Co-op cosponsors lectures, seminars, focus groups, forums, and other presentations on topics as wide-ranging as the future of

Aya Itagaki demonstrates Japanese culinary arts in one of the many cooking, nutrition, and health classes offered by the Co-op. Like most cooperatives, education is a primary commitment of the Hanover Co-op.

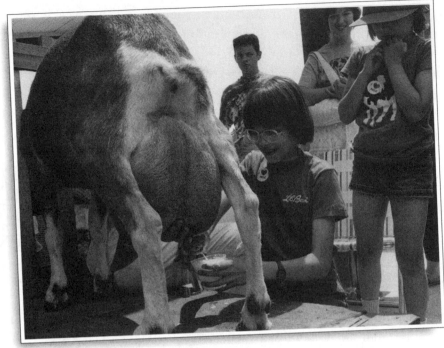

The next generation experiences the rewards and tribulations of obtaining fresh milk at the annual Dairy Day festival. By supporting local farmers and suppliers, the Co-op helps maintain a healthy rural community.

agriculture in northern New England, songbirds and coffee-growing practices, and osteoporosis.

Reflecting its Depression-era beginnings, the Hanover Consumer Cooperative Society runs full-service supermarkets rather than natural food stores. This means the stores carry everything from organic produce to cigarettes. Rather than choosing what its member-owners may buy at their stores, the Co-op's philosophy is to educate shoppers about products so they can make informed choices. Controversial items such as swordfish, snack foods made with olestra, or dairy products containing recombinant bovine growth hormone (rBGH) are not pulled from the shelves. Instead, members are given information about both sides of the controversy and allowed to choose with their dollars.

On the other hand, merchandising and marketing is governed by an awareness of member concerns. While the Co-op continues to sell cigarettes, swordfish, and olestra snacks, it does not advertise them or put them on special sale. Sugar-laden cereals are kept above children's eye-level, and no candy or other sweets are displayed in the check-out lanes. The Co-op supports local farms and producers by purchasing direct from as many as possible. Products from area bakers and food producers are found throughout the stores.

Fourteen area farms bring fresh produce in season to the Co-op stores; several more sell plants and cut flowers through the stores' floral departments. Education materials continuously stress the importance of supporting local growers. Through signs, samplings, brochures, and *Co-op News* articles, Co-op shoppers are urged to purchase locally first, regionally second, and nationally third. This means that a New Hampshire–grown apple would be chosen over a New York State apple, which would be purchased before a Washington State apple.

Supporting local farmers benefits both the shopper and the community in ways that may not be immediately apparent. Obviously, buying from local farmers encourages them to stay in business, thereby maintaining the rural landscape we all enjoy. In areas that rely on tourist trade, this is crucial. Prospering farmers also contribute to the economy of their community through the local businesses they patronize and the taxes they pay. They enrich the lives of those around them by providing a learning experience about where food comes from, and by preserving our agricultural heritage. Keeping their land open helps offset the environmental impact of increased urbanization and preserves wildlife habitat.

Locally grown food is of higher quality than food that has traveled long distances. Immediately upon harvest, the natural plant processes of respiration (oxygen exchange) and transpiration (water loss) begin to cause nutrient loss, weight loss, and changes in flavor and texture of vegetables and fruit. While temperature and humidity control can slow these processes, they cannot stop it, and the farther produce travels before it reaches the consumer, the greater the degradation.

Increased storage times also encourage the proliferation of molds, yeasts, and bacteria that cause spoilage. Long-distance shippers of produce prolong shelf life by treating their fruits and vegetables with postharvest fungicides, waxes, shellacs, and other chemicals. Growers selling to a local market have no need for postharvest chemicals.

Knowing who produces our food allows us to question and to influence how the food is grown. The customer who is concerned about pesticides can convey that concern to the local farmer who wishes to sell her corn, an opportunity that is lost when food from an anonymous source arrives from across the country. Owners of small farms are more likely to diversify and to respond to pests and diseases in creative, environmentally conscious ways than are large, monocropping agribusinesses. By choosing to support organic growers and those using integrated pest management (IPM), we encourage and empower them in their quest to farm responsibly. Likewise, the shopper wishing to avoid genetically modified foods, such as dairy products from cows receiving recombinant bovine growth hormone, can more easily find unaltered products when dealing with small family farms.

Finally, purchasing from local growers and producers reduces the amount of fossil fuels used to transport our food. It improves air quality, water quality, energy costs, and congestion.

To increase community awareness and familiarity with local agriculture, the Co-op holds two annual events—Dairy Day in June (see the photo on page 20) and Harvest Festival in August—which bring farm animals, local producers, and community members together for a day of free food and fun. The Co-op also provides land for the local farmers' market as well as community garden plots for members who need gardening space. Members and shoppers can find information at the Co-op about local farms engaged in Community Supported Agriculture (CSA). CSAs provide fresh produce directly to subscribers who, in turn, share the financial risks of farming by prepaying before the growing season begins.

Community members of all ages, from seniors to schoolchildren, share the joys of fresh produce through the Harvest Partners program. Vegetables grown by Co-op members, residents of the Kendal At Hanover retirement community, and students at Dartmouth College supply the local food banks.

Through the efforts of its education department, the Co-op supports area food banks in several ways. Annual month-long food drives in both stores provide thousands of pounds of nonperishable items to food banks in Hanover and Lebanon, New Hampshire. Each summer volunteer gardeners, headed by the Co-op's member and community outreach coordinator, grow hundreds of pounds of vegetables on Co-op land to give to the banks. All year round, volunteers pick up produce and day-old baked goods from the food stores to deliver to a number of sites in the area.

In addition to a patronage refund based on individual spending at the Co-op's stores and service center, Co-op members also benefit from

Rosemary Fifield shares her favorite family recipes through the "What's For Supper?" program. Every Thursday, shoppers can pick up a recipe card and all the ingredients for a healthy and delicious meal to prepare in less than half an hour. To enjoy these yourself, turn the page!

the opportunity to collectively purchase seeds, tubers, and soil amendments from the Fedco Seed Company each year, as well as receiving discounts on cooking classes, infant carseat rentals, *Consumer Reports* magazine, and some types of insurance. And, true to its Rochdale ancestor, the Co-op provides its members with a lending library of books and video tapes on cooperative issues, nutrition, cooking, food safety, food politics, and the environment.

The Hanover Co-op's "What's for Supper?" program is just one of many innovative education department activities, but it has proven to be one of the most popular. It is with great pleasure that we share these favorite recipes with you.

working with the Recipes

C OOKING THE FOLLOWING RECIPES in approximately 30 minutes will require some planning to make sure you are working most efficiently. Begin by reading the recipe all the way through. Note which ingredients need to be peeled, chopped, minced, or otherwise prepared as described in the list of ingredients. The text of the recipe will not repeat those details. If the recipe includes pasta, be sure to start the pasta water before proceeding with the remainder of the recipe. When cooking couscous, rice, bulgur, or other grain, time it to finish with the rest of the dish even though the recipe may begin with a description of how to cook the couscous or grain. As an alternative, be prepared to keep it warm should it finish before you are ready to eat.

Remember that the recipes in this book are meant to be guidelines, not absolutes. Modify the ingredients to suit the tastes of your family. If no one will eat cilantro, substitute fresh parsley or basil. Use fresh vegetables in season, and choose local produce whenever possible. Consider substituting polenta in either its long- or quick-cooking forms for rice or couscous, and don't be bound by the suggested shapes of pasta. Experiment with wild rice when time allows, and for optimal nutrition, replace white rice with brown, or try some of the exotic combination rice mixes on the market today.

If you're feeding dyed-in-the-wool meat eaters, don't avoid the vegetarian recipes; add small amounts of chicken, turkey, ham, or lean beef to satisfy their needs while introducing more vegetables, grains, and legumes to their diet. Likewise, the flavor combinations in the recipes using meat, poultry, or seafood will be just as interesting if you prefer to leave out animal products or replace them with tofu, tempeh, or beans.

Because these recipes represent the way *I* cook, they do not include meals based on soy products. (I thank Pam Oppenheimer for contributing the one recipe that does include silken tofu.) There is nothing judgmental about this, nor is it an oversight. Many fine books have been written on cooking with soy products, and I claim no expertise in that area.

Nutrition Information

The recipe sheets originally offered as part of the "What's for Supper?" program included nutrition information about the dish being sampled. I have eliminated that information from this book for several reasons.

Printed nutrition information reflects analysis of a recipe based on parameters established for each ingredient. Actual nutritional content of a cooked dish depends on the nutritional quality of the ingredients used and on how closely one followed the recipe. I would rather encourage substitution and innovation than strict adherence to a list of ingredients.

Second, I don't wish to encourage those who mistakenly overemphasize the importance of the nutritional content of a single meal, rather than considering the impact of their eating habits overall. It's perfectly fine to eat a meal in which the calories from fat exceed the American Heart Association's recommendation of 30 percent of total calories, as long as one *averages* no more than 30 percent of calories from fat in the total diet. Too often, when handing out samples of a "What's for Supper?" recipe, I would hear, "I thought these recipes were healthy. How can they contain cheese?" Yet cheese contributes more than just fat and calories; cheese adds flavor and serves as a source of calcium, protein, and vitamin D. Furthermore, the small amounts of calories and fat from cheese are offset by the low-fat, low-calorie nature of the vegetables, legumes, and grains they accompany.

Of greater importance than the amount of fat one eats is the nature of that fat. Both saturated and unsaturated fats contain the same number of fat calories, yet the former is much worse for one's health than the latter. Unhealthy trans-fatty acids, found in hardened vegetable oils such as margarine and shortening, are not included in standard nutrition analysis. Our obsession with fat numbers can lead us to overlook the much more important fact that a diet based on fresh produce, grains, and beans, cooked in olive or canola oil, and seasoned with small amounts of a highly flavored cheese or lean meat or seafood will always be healthful.

Finally, I consider eating to be one of the major pleasures in life, and fear of food to be a tragedy. Instead of eating by the numbers, we should cultivate good eating habits and an appreciation for quality food. I believe these recipes achieve both.

Having said this, I will add that, due to popular demand, all of the recipes in this book are designed to produce a serving that provides no more than 30 percent of total calories from fat and no more than 10 percent of total calories from saturated fat. Unless high-sodium stock and canned products are used, sodium content per serving is generally less than 500 milligrams. Dishes containing animal products average a cholesterol content between 30 and 75 milligrams per serving as long as the portions used closely resemble those called for in the recipe and do not become the main ingredient.

Ingredients

Choosing ingredients and cooking them properly is an important part of producing a nutritious and healthful dish. The nature of the fats, the quality of the produce, and the freshness of ingredients are fundamental to creating meals that taste good and are good for you as well.

OILS

The two most healthful oils for cooking are olive and canola. Both are high in heart-healthy monounsaturated fats.

Olive oil on the American market comes in two forms: "extra-virgin" and what used to be called "pure" but is now simply designated as

Saving Time in the Kitchen

KITCHEN ARRANGEMENT

Make sure food, utensils, and equipment are arranged conveniently for fast-paced but safe work.

Use time-saving equipment such as microwaves, toaster ovens, pressure cookers, electric frying pans, and other small appliances that cook food quickly and efficiently. Vegetables are a natural for cooking in a microwave. They lose fewer nutrients and cook quickly. Microwaves also make quick and tasty desserts of fruits such as apples and pears.

Use your food processor only when the clean-up time is offset by a sufficient amount of vegetables or other ingredients to be processed. Consider processing extra to freeze in small portions to improve the efficiency of time spent cleaning the machine.

When possible, use one all-purpose container to mix, cook, serve, and store leftovers. One-dish meals save clean-up time.

PANTRY SUPPLIES

Keep your food cabinets, refrigerator, and freezer stocked with quick-to-fix ingredients that can be used in a variety of ways. Remember, you can prepare nutritious, delicious meals in a minimum of time without resorting to processed foods.

Keep a supply of rice, quick-cooking grains, and dry pasta in the cupboard. Include aromatic rice varieties such as jasmine, white basmati, and Texmati, which offer added flavor and interest while cooking in just 15 minutes, and quick-cooking long-grain brown rice, now available from Minute Rice. Quinoa, millet, bulgur, and kasha (buckwheat) are whole grains that cook within 30 minutes and can be used in place of rice in most recipes. An assortment of pasta shapes, including couscous, makes eating fun and provides a change in texture, flavor, and visual appeal.

A good selection of canned beans such as kidney, cannellini, pinto, black, and chickpeas (garbanzos), makes it easy to add nutrition and substance to a fast and easy meal. Choose low-sodium, organically grown beans whenever possible, and when you have time, cook your own dried beans from scratch and freeze in pint containers for use in single recipes.

 Frozen vegetables, fish fillets and fish steaks, chicken breasts or legs, turkey cutlets, or lean ground meats can be thawed as needed. Freeze ground meats as a large flattened "burger" for quick thawing.

 Canned tuna or salmon packed in water is a versatile food that is nutritious as well as tasty.

 Canned tomatoes do not lose nutrients in processing and have better flavor than out-of-season tomatoes. Use fresh, ripe tomatoes when they are at their most flavorful, and freeze some for winter use.

 Keep a supply of commonly used flavoring ingredients such as onions, garlic, Parmesan cheese, and dried herbs. Bouillon cubes or powder can be used to make a cup of stock when needed as an ingredient.

 Flavorful sauces such as tamari and Worcestershire, salsas, and prepared horseradish and mustards are quick and easy additions that perk up simple foods.

PLAN AHEAD

 Plan some meals in advance, defrosting foods ahead of time, and shopping with a meal in mind.

 Make extra on weekends and freeze meal-sized portions for the rest of the week.

 Double your meat loaf recipe and freeze half of the uncooked mixture for future use as meatballs or for stuffing peppers or other vegetables.

 Cook a chicken and freeze portions for those recipes that call for cooked chicken or leftover cooked meats.

Keep a shopping list handy to note the items you use up or will need for the recipe you're planning to make.

Collect quick and easy menus and recipes, like those in this collection, and use them to keep your meals easy to make and interesting to eat.

"olive oil." Extra-virgin olive oil is from the first cold pressing of the olive and is the highest quality olive oil available. Like wine, the flavor, aroma, and color of extra-virgin olive oil varies, based on the variety of olive, stage of maturity at harvest, where the olives were grown, environmental conditions, and how the olives were handled. Extra-virgin olive oils range from delicate and fruity to full-bodied and peppery, and from pale gold to a rich deep green. Because it is more expensive, extra-virgin olive oil is best used where its flavor and aroma can be enjoyed, on salads, drizzled in soups, and as a flavoring for pasta or crusty bread. With its naturally high vitamin E content, extra-virgin olive oil will keep at room temperature for up to two years if shielded from light and excessive heat.

Olive oil that is not designated as "extra-virgin" has the same concentration of monounsaturated fats, but has been refined with heat and chemicals to produce a basically tasteless oil. Refinement gives it a higher smoking point and a lower price, and this type of olive oil is best used for sautéing and frying. Some olive oils have had their flavor enhanced by a small amount of extra-virgin olive oil. Those that have not remain bland and tasteless and are sometimes designated as "light" olive oil. Be aware that this refers to flavor and aroma only. All olive oils have the same number of calories and the same amount of fat. Refined olive oils should be shielded from light and heat and used within a year. If refrigerated, olive oil will solidify, but will liquefy once it returns to room temperature.

Canola oil is pressed from the seeds of a member of the mustard family known as rape. The term "canola" was coined to give the oil a more appealing name than "rapeseed oil" and is an acronym for "Canadian oil, low acid," since most canola is a product of Canada. Canola is low in saturated fat, high in monounsaturated fat, and also contains the healthful omega-3 fatty acid, linoleic acid. It is tasteless and best used for sautéing, frying, and as an ingredient in baked goods and pancakes.

My personal preference for sautéing is extra-virgin olive oil since it is not refined with chemicals. However, in this book I only designate extra-virgin olive oil in those recipes that require its distinctive flavor. All other recipes, except those with an Asian influence (where peanut or sesame oil may be used to produce a more authentic flavor), simply call for olive oil. In all of these recipes, feel free to substitute canola oil, if you prefer.

HERBS

Recipes in this book that include herbs generally offer a choice between dried herbs and fresh. Drying herbs concentrates their flavor, making it necessary to use only about one-third of the amount designated for the fresh form of the same herb. Dried herbs are easy to store and simple to use; however it is also easy to keep them too long so that they lose their potency and have a flavor akin to dust. If you have the option to purchase dried herbs from bulk bins rather than in premeasured jars, do so. Not only can you buy an amount you will use in a short period of time, but the cost per pound is unbelievably cheaper when you are not paying for the container and the cost of filling and transporting it. Buy dried herbs in small amounts, and keep them tightly wrapped in small plastic bags or containers with a minimum of airspace. Be sure to label them clearly, since they tend to look similar.

Cooking with fresh herbs is a sensual pleasure, especially when working with basil, thyme, tarragon, rosemary, mint, and dill. I find fresh oregano too variable in flavor, although it is always aromatic. Never use dried cilantro, and purchase fresh flat-leaf Italian parsley whenever possible, as it is superior to curly parsley and light-years away from dried.

Mince or chop basil more efficiently by stacking the leaves before beginning to chop. Strip tarragon, rosemary, and thyme leaves from their woody stems before chopping. Thyme leaves are often small enough to be left whole. Rosemary, on the other hand, can be unpleasantly twiglike if not minced. When using a bay leaf, always leave it whole, and be sure to remove the bay leaf before serving the dish. Bay

■ ■ ■

leaves will never soften and have been known to cut the esophagus if swallowed.

Dried herbs are generally added earlier in the cooking than fresh herbs. Dried herbs need time to soften and to release their flavors, while fresh herbs can be overcooked to the point of losing flavor or turning bitter. In these recipes, if the fresh herb is cooked no longer than 15 minutes, I have not differentiated between when to add dried versus fresh herbs.

MUSHROOMS

Cultivated and exotic mushrooms are fun to work with and provide texture and flavor variety when used separately or together. Standard white button mushrooms are the most familiar; interestingly, their brown counterpart, the cremini, was once the standard mushroom available in grocery stores. Today the brown mushroom is considered an exotic and sells for up to six times the price of its white cousin. A portabella (or portobello) is simply an overgrown cremini that has fully opened.

Shiitake, enoki, and oyster mushrooms round out the types most commonly available today. The stem of the shiitake remains tough when cooked and should be removed before use. I like to save them in a container in the freezer until I have enough to make a flavorful stock. The oyster can also have a tough stem where the clusters join at the base, and these should be removed and saved for stock.

Mushrooms that are closed and have no gills showing can be washed under running water or wiped clean with a wet paper towel. Open-gilled mushrooms such as portabella and shiitake should not be soaked or exposed to excessive amounts of water, as they will absorb and give back that water through their gills. Wipe these mushrooms clean with a wet paper towel. Briefly rinse oyster and enoki mushrooms under running water and pat dry.

When they are available, don't be afraid to replace the mushrooms in these recipes with wild types such as chanterelles, boletes, or morels.

■ ■ ■

TAMARI AND SOY SAUCE

Tamari and soy sauce are Asian condiments traditionally made from fermented soybeans, salt, and water. In addition, soy sauce contains roasted cracked wheat. Few mass-marketed soy sauces are made in the traditional manner, however. Instead, they contain soy extract, hydrolyzed vegetable protein, preservatives, and sometimes, corn syrup. People sensitive to monosodium glutamate (MSG) should avoid hydrolyzed vegetable protein, as it is high in glutamate. All soy sauces and tamari are high in sodium, containing around 1,200 and 900 milligrams per tablespoon, respectively. "Light" or reduced-sodium soy sauces contain 500 to 600 milligrams.

Tamari is the soy sauce of choice used in the recipes in this book. However, regular soy sauce, *shoyu* (Japanese soy sauce), or light soy sauce can be used in place of tamari.

STOCK

The term "stock" is used in these recipes to designate either stock, broth, or bouillon. Two types of stock—vegetable and chicken—can be used interchangeably unless you are making a strictly vegetarian dish, in which you will want to use only vegetable stock.

The flavor, fat, and sodium content of canned broth varies among brands, although it is now possible to purchase low-fat, low-sodium chicken broth. I have yet to find a canned vegetable broth that isn't harsh and tending toward sweet, but several good vegetarian broth powders are available. Bouillon cubes are high in sodium, and should be a last resort.

Making stock from scratch is not difficult, but is obviously something to be done when you have the extra time. Vegetable stock should cook for no more than an hour; chicken stock will benefit from two or more hours on the stove. I like to save odds and ends for stock by putting them in the freezer; don't use old or spoiled vegetables that you would normally throw away. Remember that you will be straining out the solids, so feel free to use any clean parts you might not normally eat, such as shiitake mushroom stems, corn cobs, chard stems, potato parings, celery root skins, and trimmings from leeks, asparagus, fennel, celery, parsnips, green beans, and winter squash. I also save the rinds from Parmesan cheese for use in stocks intended for bean dishes. When making stock, avoid members of the brassica family (cabbage, cauliflower, broccoli, and Brussels sprouts) as well as turnips, rutabagas, beets, onion skins, and artichokes, all of which can impart unpleasant flavors to stock.

Vegetable stock. Always chop the vegetables into small chunks to create more surface area for extraction of flavors. Include those baby carrots that have dried up in the vegetable drawer, plus any open mushroom caps and the zucchini for which you can't find a home. Then start with a slow (5 to 10 minute) sauté of 1 large onion, 2 celery ribs with leaves, 6 smashed garlic cloves, and 2 carrots in 1 tablespoon of olive oil in a large stock pot. Add 6 to 8 sprigs each of fresh thyme and parsley, and 1 or 2 bay leaves. I find other herbs a bit tricky, as it's easy to turn a stock bitter with rosemary, marjoram, or basil. Stir in the remaining chopped vegetables from your freezer or refrigerator drawers, and cook for another 5 minutes. Add 2 quarts of cold water and 2 teaspoons of salt. Mix well and bring to a boil, then lower heat and simmer, uncovered, for 30 minutes.

Turn off the heat and let the contents of the pot settle for a few minutes. Set a sieve over a large container, and strain the soup through the sieve. Do not let the cooked vegetables and herbs sit in the finished stock, as they will make it bitter. Taste the strained stock, and if it seems weak, return it to the heat, bring it to a boil, lower the heat, and simmer to reduce the volume and concentrate the flavors. Or, taste the strained stock, and add miso, tamari, or soy sauce, by the spoonful, tasting after each addition until the stock meets your expectations. Remember, however, that these ingredients will also add significant amounts of sodium. Cool the stock in shallow, refrigerated containers, then store in 1- or 2-cup portions in the freezer.

Chicken stock. Unless you have access to the plump old fowl that makes the best stock, you will probably need to use a roasting chicken. Or freeze uncooked necks, backs, and wings from frying chickens until you have enough to turn into stock. Always start with cold water to slowly draw out all of the chicken flavor.

Into a heavy stockpot or soup kettle, put 4 to 5 pounds of chicken parts, 2 medium-sized onions cut into cubes, 1 large carrot cut into cubes, 4 crushed garlic cloves, one sprig of fresh thyme, and 1/2 cup chopped Italian parsley. Add 10 cups of cold water, more if necessary to cover the ingredients. Slowly bring the liquid to a simmer over medium heat, skimming off and discarding the foam that rises to the top. When the foam stops forming, cover the pot, and keep at a slow simmer for 1 1/2 hours or longer, until the chicken is thoroughly cooked and is starting to fall off the bones. Strain the stock through a fine sieve or a double layer of cheesecloth, and discard the vegetables and herbs. Retain the cooked chicken meat for another dish, if desired; it will provide more substance than flavor at this point. Add salt and pepper to taste, then refrigerate the stock in several shallow containers until the fat cools and solidifies at the top. Remove the fat with a slotted spoon, divide the stock into 1- or 2-cup containers, and freeze until needed.

COOKING DRIED BEANS

While canned beans are now available in organic and low-sodium versions, the best flavor and texture is still to be had from dried beans you cook yourself. In addition, working with dried beans is a satisfying experience that begins with the pleasure of handling and admiring the beauty of beans in their natural state. Once cooked, many beans lose their distinguishing markings and unique colors, but there is nothing mundane about a dried Vermont cranberry bean or the American heirloom known as Jacob's Cattle. Starting with the uncooked bean also means having a much wider variety of beans at your disposal than when you restrict yourself to canned.

Always begin by sorting dried beans, as it is not unusual to find small bits of earth and tiny stones mixed in. I find this easiest to achieve by spreading them in a single layer on a cookie sheet with edges. Remove any beans that are chipped, cracked, shriveled, or split—all signs of old beans that will need to cook for an excessive amount of time in order to soften. After sorting, rinse the beans well.

Cooking times for beans vary with their age, size, and variety, and with the hardness of the water in which they are cooked, as well as the altitude at which you are cooking. Consider cooking beans in a pressure cooker, which will save energy as well as time. Allow about one-third the amount of time needed to cook them on the stovetop or in the oven. Beans cooked in a pressure cooker do not need to be soaked.

Soaking beans shortens their cooking time and removes some of the complex carbohydrates that are responsible for the intestinal discomfort beans can cause, especially in those people who don't eat them regularly. During the soaking period, the beans will absorb water and swell to two to three times their original size. Lentils and split peas do not need to be soaked before cooking.

Beans can be soaked by either a long or short method. The long method involves covering beans with water at least four times their volume and letting them sit for at least 4 hours. In most cases, this can be done at room temperature, although in extremely hot weather, they may begin to ferment. Many cooks choose to do this overnight.

For a quicker soak, place the sorted and rinsed beans in a large saucepan or Dutch oven and cover them with 4 times their volume of cold water. Cover and bring to a boil, boil 1 minute, remove from the heat, and allow to stand for 1 hour.

Drain the beans soaked by either method, discarding the soaking water, which will contain sugars that cause indigestion. Cover the beans with fresh water in a large saucepan or Dutch oven and bring to a rolling boil. Boil hard for 5 minutes, then lower the heat and cook at a simmer. Do not add salt or acidic ingredients such as tomatoes, wine, or vinegar until the beans are tender but not yet fully cooked. (Bite-test the beans after 30 minutes.) Adding these ingredients too soon can toughen the beans and prolong their cooking time. If you choose to add garlic, onions, or herbs to your cooking beans, these can be included from the beginning.

In general, soaked beans will take about 1½ hours to cook, whether on top of the stove or in the oven. If you are cooking them in the oven, bring to a boil as described above, then discard the boiling water and put the drained beans into a baking dish or casserole. Add boiling water to cover, then cover the container. Bake at 325° to 350°F (163° to 177°C), adding salt or acid at the end as described above, and keep them simmering rather than boiling. Beans are perfectly cooked when they are soft and creamy inside with intact skins. They can also be made in a slow cooker for 6 to 8 hours on high or low heat, respectively.

Cooked beans can be frozen in small portions to be used in these recipes upon demand.

Lentils used in *The Co-op Cookbook* recipes do not need to be precooked.

COOKING PASTA AND GRAINS

The majority of our quick and easy one-dish meals are served on, or include, a grain-based product such as pasta, rice, quinoa, bulgur, or Asian noodles. Grains make up the base of the USDA Food Guide Pyramid, providing complex carbohydrates for long-term energy. Whole grains also contain B vitamins and fiber and are filling and satisfying without being high in calories.

Grains in combinations with legumes are part of all traditional diets, with the combination of rice and beans being the most universal. Wheat-based pastas and couscous, as well as bulgur, are quick to cook and go well with a variety of flavors, while quinoa, millet, and kasha (roasted buckwheat) offer interesting alternatives to rice. Asian noodles, with their unique flavors and textures, can be used in place of pasta in any recipe. For individuals who wish to avoid wheat, pastas are also made from rice, quinoa, kamut, corn, amaranth, and spelt.

■ ■ ■

Nonwheat pastas tend to have a crumbly texture and to fall apart when over-cooked. Artichoke pastas are made from Jerusalem artichoke flour, and generally contain wheat as well.

Many of the *The Co-op Cookbook* recipes begin with cooking the grain in a separate pan. The following information is a general guideline to easy preparation of each type.

Pasta should be cooked in plenty of rapidly boiling water. To salt or not to salt the water is strictly a personal preference; very little salt actually remains on the pasta. There is no point to adding oil to pasta water. The oil remains on top of the water and has no effect on the boiling pasta itself. It is then poured out and down the drain. Pasta should not be rinsed after cooking unless it is going to be used in a salad. Rather, leave a small amount of the hot pasta water with the pasta until you are ready to add it to the dish or serve it. Stir the pasta, then drain and proceed.

Timing on pasta is always approximate. Different brands and different shapes and sizes cook differently. Therefore, it's best to use the recommended time on the box only as an estimate, and to begin to bite-test the pasta a few minutes before you expect it to be done. Pasta should be taken from the cooking water when it is still slightly more chewy than you wish it to be, as it will continue to cook and soften over the next few minutes. For pasta purchased in bulk without instructions, begin to taste-test when it is no longer translucent but begins to look opaque; for medium shapes such as rotini and penne, this is generally somewhere between 8 and 11 minutes.

Asian noodles can be made from wheat, rice, mung beans, buckwheat, or other starches. Some are soaked rather than cooked, and all are ready when tender, not al dente. Drain and rinse, then use the noodles in the recipe as indicated.

Soak cellophane (bean-thread) noodles or rice sticks in a bowl of warm water for 15 to 30 minutes. Cover wide rice noodles with boiling water, and let them soften. Chinese egg noodles come in several widths and are cooked in boiling water until soft. They often need to be pulled apart with chopsticks as they cook. All will be cooked within 10 to 15 minutes.

Japanese soba, udon, and somen noodles require a special technique to cook properly. Add the noodles to plenty of boiling water, return to a boil, and add cold water to make the boil subside. Do this three or four times, until the noodles are done. Depending on the thickness of the noodles, this should take approximately 5 to 7 minutes. Drain, rinse, and use in the dish as the recipe indicates.

White rice is cooked in twice its own volume of water; that is, 1 cup rice to 2 cups water. Do not salt the water. Stir well, then cover and bring to a boil. Lower the heat and simmer, covered and undisturbed, for 15 to 20 minutes. The water should be completely absorbed. Let the rice sit for an additional 5 minutes, covered, then fluff with a fork before serving or adding to the dish.

Brown rice is more nutritious than white rice, which has had the nutrient-rich bran layer polished off. Brown rice takes about 45 minutes to cook on the stovetop, and requires 2⅛ cups water to 1 cup of brown rice. Bring the water to a boil in a saucepan, add the rice, lower the heat, and cover the pan. Cook over low heat for 40 to 50 minutes, until the grains are tender and the water has been absorbed.

If you have a pressure cooker, you can cook brown rice in 20 minutes. Combine 1 cup rice with 2 cups water, 1 tablespoon oil, and a few pinches of salt in the pressure cooker. Bring the pressure to high, then lower the heat to maintain it, and cook for 20 minutes. Turn off the heat, and quick-release for long-grain rice, or let the pressure drop on its own for short-grain rice. Brown rice cooked in a pressure cooker will be slightly stickier than that cooked on the stovetop.

Instant brown rice is now available and has the same nutritional value as long-cooking brown rice. Follow package directions for the amount to use per serving and how to cook it, which takes approximately 15 minutes.

■ ■ ■

Wild rice is actually a grass rather than a rice, and because it is laborious to harvest, it is more expensive. It expands significantly when cooked, however, which helps offset the extra cost, and is more flavorful and nutritious than true rice. It is best to clean wild rice by soaking it in water to cover, which allows chaff and other debris to float to the surface. Drain the rice, and add 1 cup of wild rice to 1 quart of boiling water in a saucepan. Lower the heat, cover, and cook for 45 to 50 minutes. When the rice is ready, it will be tender but should still have a bit of resistance, and many of the grains may have split. Pour off any extra water, cover, and let stand for 5 minutes before serving.

Couscous is a pasta, not a grain. It comes in both whole wheat and refined wheat (French) forms. Couscous available in this country is precooked and needs only to be reconstituted with boiling water. For fluffy couscous, use 1¼ cups of water per cup of couscous or follow the recipe directions. Boil the water and add it to the couscous; cover the bowl and let it sit for 5 minutes or until the water is absorbed. Fluff it with a fork. Couscous absorbs flavors well and can be reconstituted with broth or juice as well.

Bulgur is precooked wheat and comes in several sizes of cracked kernels. It needs to be cooked from the heat in boiling water. Add 1½ cups of boiling water to 1 cup of bulgur and let sit for 20 minutes, covered, until the water is absorbed and the bulgur is ready to eat.

Quinoa (pronounced "keen-wah") is a grain that was once the staple food of the Incas; it is close to a complete protein in its amino acid content. Quinoa has a bitter natural coating that needs to be rinsed off. Rinse it in a colander or strainer with cold water, then drain and cook like rice.

Millet is cooked in 2 to 3 cups of water or broth per cup of grain and takes 20 to 30 minutes to cook. If you have the time, lightly toasting millet in a dry skillet before cooking adds to its flavor.

Kasha, or roasted buckwheat groats, should be quickly coated and cooked with egg whites before adding liquid. This keeps the kernels from sticking together. Cook as rice, but check at 10 minutes for water absorption and doneness.

PEELING AND SEEDING TOMATOES

Not all tomatoes need to be peeled and seeded. Italian, plum-shaped tomatoes can generally be used as is, after being washed and stemmed. Other varieties may have tough skins or contain excessive liquid and will benefit from having the skins, seeds, and the jelly surrounding the seeds removed. To do so, cut a shallow X on the bottom (blossom end) of the tomato with a paring knife. Drop the tomato into boiling water for 10 to 15 seconds, or until the cut skin begins to curl. Remove from the water with a slotted spoon or strainer, cool, and peel away the skin. Cut in half and scoop out the jelly and seeds with your finger. Chop or dice the remaining tomato flesh.

ROASTING PEPPERS

Roasting red bell peppers intensifies their flavor, softens them, and allows for peeling. Peppers can be roasted over a gas burner, a grill, or under the broiler. Choose peppers with thick flesh and smooth surfaces, devoid of deep crevices. Wash well. Roast the peppers over or under direct heat until the skin becomes charred, turning them with tongs to make sure all surfaces are blackened. To roast several peppers at once, line a broiler pan with aluminum foil and lay the peppers on the surface. Cook under the broiler, turning until completely blackened. Remove from the broiler, fold up the edges of the foil to form a sealed package, and allow the peppers to steam inside for 15 minutes. Or, remove the peppers to a bowl, cover, and allow to steam. This will loosen the charred skins and finish cooking the flesh.

Remove the peppers from their steam chamber and peel away the loosened bits of skin, using your hand or a paper towel. Do not rinse them under running water, as you will lose much of the flavor. A little

■ ■ ■

skin left behind is not a problem. Cut the pepper in half, remove the seeds and membranes, then slice the pepper into strips. To store, place in a clean container, cover with olive oil, and refrigerate for up to a week. Reserve the sweet juices that drain from the pepper during roasting, steaming, and peeling to add flavor to the dish you are preparing or use as an ingredient in a vinaigrette.

Keeping Food Safe

As consumers, we need to take a more active role in ensuring the safety of the food we eat and serve. Foodborne illness, caused by mishandling of perishable foods from farm to fork, is on the rise. In part, this is because the nature of foodborne illness is changing, and those practices that were once acceptable can no longer be considered safe.

For instance, prior to the mid-1980s, homemakers could assume that intact eggs were safe, and that only cracked eggs were at risk for contamination by *Salmonella* bacteria. This changed when researchers found *Salmonella enteriditis* in the oviducts of laying hens, indicating potential contamination of eggs before the shell developed. Those of us who made eggnog at home, used raw eggs in French silk pie, or were in the habit of licking the beaters after mixing a chocolate cake had to change our habits.

With the advent of *E. coli* O157:H7, commonly called the "hamburger bacteria," the United States Department of Agriculture (USDA) warned consumers to cook their hamburgers well. Within a few short years, dangerous bacteria began to appear on produce and in apple juice. Today, supermarkets are required to post warning signs about *Salmonella* on fresh sprouts and *E. coli* in unpasteurized apple cider. During the same time period, *Campylobacter* and *Listeria* joined the lexicon of dangerous foodborne bacteria that were previously unknown or that caused illness only in live animals. Today, *Campylobacter,* found on poultry, is the number-one cause of foodborne illness in the United States, and *Listeria* has become a dangerous contaminant of deli meats and ready-to-eat cold foods.

■   ■   ■

Our modern system of food production and distribution also puts us at greater risk. At one time, a mishandled side of beef might affect the health of only a few families who purchased that meat from a local slaughterhouse. In the summer of 1998, thirty-five million pounds of ground beef were recalled from coast to coast because of potential *E. coli* contamination in one packing plant.

Foodborne illness is more than flu-like symptoms that bring discomfort for a few hours; it has the potential to cause serious disease and even death. *Campylobacter* has been implicated in cases of Guillian-Barré Syndrome, a paralytic disease. *Listeria* can cause meningitis and miscarriages. Four segments of our population are at particular risk from foodborne bacteria: small children, pregnant women, the elderly, and those with weakened immune systems.

Our best protection from foodborne illness is to become knowledgeable, conscientious handlers of perishable foods. We can begin by washing our hands often when handling food. Always wash your hands before you begin, and after any interruptions such as answering the phone, hugging a child, or wiping your nose. Cover all open sores and cuts on your hands and arms with a bandage. Wash your hands immediately after handling raw meats or eggs.

Wash all produce, including items such as melons, before cutting or eating. Soilborne bacteria on the outside of melon rinds, for instance, will be drawn into the edible portion by the knife. Wash all herbs before using, and be especially fastidious about removing soil from lettuce leaves and other produce that will not be cooked. Foods that are grown organically are no safer than any other from soilborne bacteria; don't be lulled into thinking you don't need to wash it because it is organic or because you grew it yourself.

Keep separate cutting boards for raw animal products and foods that will not be cooked before eating. Make sure everyone in your household knows which are which. The debate continues as to whether plastic or wooden cutting boards are easier to keep clean. Of greater importance is making sure that the surface of your cutting board is not

■ ■ ■

overly scarred with crevices that will trap and hold food particles and bacteria. Wash utensils in hot soapy water after using them to cut or mix raw animal products and before using them on foods that will not be cooked.

Be aware that bacteria multiply rapidly at room temperature, and always keep cold foods cold and hot foods hot. One of the best investments you can make is an instant-read thermometer. Use it to ensure that hamburgers reach 165°F (74°C) and seafood reaches 140°F (60°C). Cook chicken until there is no pink flesh and the juices run clear and colorless.

When cooking or reheating foods in a microwave, always stir partway through, because microwave cooking is not consistent and can leave cold or lukewarm spots. Heat food thoroughly, and if it's not hot, return it to the stove or microwave until it is.

Put away leftovers as soon as possible. Refrigerate hot foods such as soups and stews in shallow containers to make sure they reach cold temperatures quickly; never let them cool at room temperature. Thaw frozen foods in the refrigerator or in a container of cold water, not on the countertop.

Many people erroneously believe that mayonnaise is the culprit in summertime food poisonings from potato, macaroni, or other salads. While mayonnaise is a common ingredient among them, it is also too acidic to support bacterial growth. The dangerous part of these salads is the cooked protein source—potatoes, pasta, eggs, chicken, or seafood. Never allow the cooked ingredients to sit at room temperature for long periods of time just because the mayonnaise has not been added. Refrigerate all cooked foods as soon as possible.

Keep in mind that botulism, a potentially fatal foodborne illness, occurs when foods are put into conditions where oxygen is no longer present and then kept at room temperature. Garlic cloves or basil leaves coated with oil, as in flavored olive oils, provide the perfect medium for the botulism bacteria to make their deadly toxins. Always refrigerate flavored olive oils that do not contain an acidic ingredient such as citric acid, and use them within a two-week period. When serving, pour out only what you will use—for instance, to dip baguette slices in garlic oil—and refrigerate the remainder. Discard any room-temperature left-overs at the end of the meal.

Finally, memorize this very important rhyme: When in doubt, throw it out. Many bacterial contaminants are tasteless and odorless. Never taste food that is suspect. Remember, no food item is worth the price of putting yourself or others at risk from dangerous foodborne illness.

．．．．．．．．．．．

Soups,
chilis, &
stews

．．．．．．．．．．．

Vegetarian

Italian Pasta and Bean Soup   SERVES 6

Using beans, vegetables, and pasta, this traditional dish brings together classic flavors in a meal that satisfies the soul as well as the body. Use two different types of beans, if you wish, and vary the macaroni shapes for added interest.

2 tsp. olive oil

2 cloves garlic, finely chopped

1 medium onion, finely chopped

2 cups diced tomatoes

1½ tsp. crushed dried or minced fresh rosemary leaves

3½ cups vegetable stock

2 cups water

4 cups cooked cannellini or garbanzo beans, drained and rinsed if canned

6 oz. medium macaroni (elbows, medium shells, penne)

½ tsp. dried oregano or 1½ tsp. minced fresh oregano

½ tsp. dried thyme or 1½ tsp. fresh thyme

½ tsp. dried basil or 1½ tsp. minced fresh basil

Freshly ground black pepper, to taste

Grated Romano or Parmesan cheese

Heat oil in a large pot over medium heat. Add garlic and onion, and cook, stirring, until golden, about 3 minutes. Add tomatoes and rosemary; simmer for 5 minutes. Pour in the stock and 2 cups water. Bring to a simmer over medium heat.

Meanwhile, in a small bowl, mash 1 cup of beans with a fork or potato masher. Stir the mashed beans into the tomato-stock mixture, along with the macaroni. Season with oregano, thyme, basil, and black pepper. Simmer, uncovered, until the macaroni is almost tender, approximately 10 minutes. Stir in the remaining beans, and heat through.

Serve the soup with a sprinkling of grated cheese.

Santa Fe Soup   SERVES 4

*Serve with warm, folded corn tortillas, crusty bread, or wedges of pita bread
to sop up all the delicious flavor.*

3 cups vegetable stock

4 cups cooked black beans,
drained and rinsed if canned

1 Tbs. olive oil

2 cloves garlic, finely chopped

1 medium onion, finely chopped

2 cups crushed tomatoes

1 cup salsa or picante sauce

8 oz. elbows, shells, or spiral
macaroni

2 tsp. chili powder, or to taste

Salt and freshly ground black
pepper, to taste

Combine 1 cup of the stock with 2 cups of black beans in a blender or
food processor, and purée until smooth. Or mash beans with a masher,
and stir in the liquid by hand.

Heat oil in a large pot over medium heat. Add garlic and onion, and
cook, stirring, for 1 minute. Add tomatoes, salsa, remaining stock, and
remaining beans. Bring to a boil, cover, and simmer over medium heat
for 5 minutes. Return the mixture to a rolling boil, and stir in the pasta.
Cook, uncovered, until the pasta is cooked but still firm to the bite (*al
dente*). Stir in the chili powder and the mashed beans, and heat through.
Taste and season as needed. If chili is too thick, adjust with water or
additional stock and serve.

Hearty Vegetable Soup

SERVES 4

This is one of those recipes where you can use what's on hand to create a fla-vorful soup tuned to the seasons. In the summer, consider eggplant cubes, and be sure to use fresh tomatoes. In the winter, cabbage and/or kale add a hearty dimension to the mix of vegetables. Replace the pasta with potatoes, if you like, or include them both, and vary the beans or leave them out. Acini di pepe is a pasta the size of peppercorns, resembling large couscous grains.

2 Tbs. olive oil

1 medium onion, coarsely chopped

2 portabella mushrooms, cubed

1 cubanelle or long Italian green pepper, coarsely chopped

1 small zucchini or yellow squash, cubed

¼ cabbage head, thinly sliced

6 cups diced tomatoes

1 cup water or vegetable stock

2 tsp. dried oregano or 2 Tbs. minced fresh oregano

2 cups cooked garbanzo beans, drained and rinsed if canned

1 cup acini di pepe, ditalini, couscous, or rice

Salt and freshly ground black pepper, to taste

Heat 1 tablespoon of the oil in a Dutch oven over medium heat. Add the onion, and cook for 3 minutes. Add the mushrooms, pepper, squash, and sliced cabbage. If the mixture seems dry, add the second tablespoon of oil. Mix well and sauté for 5 minutes, until the vegetables become tender and the cabbage wilts. Add the tomatoes, water or stock, and oregano (if using dried), and bring the mixture to a boil. Add the gar-banzo beans, and cook at a gentle simmer for 5 minutes. Bring to a rolling boil, add the pasta, mix well, and cook for 10 minutes, or until the pasta is done. If the soup appears too thick, add more water as needed. Add the fresh oregano, and mix gently. Season to taste with salt and pepper, and serve with crusty bread on the side.

Purée of White Bean Soup SERVES 4

This thick and garlicky soup is a Mediterranean classic normally made from dried beans slowly cooked with potatoes, onions, and garlic. Our quick version takes advantage of cooked beans and a food processor to produce a hearty supper dish to serve with plenty of good crusty bread.

4 cups vegetable stock, divided

1 medium potato, peeled and diced small

1 large carrot, peeled and diced small

1 Tbs. olive oil

1 medium onion, chopped

3 cloves garlic, minced

¼ tsp. dried thyme or scant tsp. fresh thyme

¼ tsp. crushed dried or minced fresh rosemary

4 cups cannellini beans, drained and rinsed if canned

Salt and freshly ground black pepper, to taste

1 tsp. lemon juice

Croutons or toasted whole wheat bread

Bring 2 cups of the stock to a boil in a large saucepan. Add potato and carrot, cover, reduce heat, and simmer gently for 15 minutes.

While potato cooks, place oil in a heavy stock pot or Dutch oven over medium-high heat. Add onion, reduce heat to low, cover, and cook for 10 minutes, stirring occasionally. Add the garlic, and cook for 1 minute. Add 1 cup of stock, and bring to a boil. Add the cooked potato, carrot, and their liquid; stir in thyme and rosemary.

In a food processor or blender, purée the beans with the final cup of stock. Add to the soup and bring to a boil. Season to taste with salt and pepper and adjust thickness with additional stock, if necessary. Stir in lemon juice. Serve with croutons or toasted bread as garnish.

Last-Minute Minestrone

SERVES 6

It's up to you what goes into this quick and hearty version of an Italian classic. The potato adds texture and flavor. Add whatever cooked or frozen vegetables you have on hand.

1 small onion, minced

2 cloves garlic, minced

6 cups vegetable stock

1 small potato, scrubbed or peeled and diced into ½-inch cubes

2 cups cooked vegetables such as green or yellow beans, carrots, corn, peas, kale, spinach, or chard

2 cups cooked garbanzo, cannellini, or red kidney beans, drained and rinsed if canned

2 cups diced tomatoes

4 ounces small pasta (ditalini, small shells, or elbows)

Freshly grated Parmesan or Romano cheese

Place minced onion and garlic in a large saucepan with ½ cup of the stock. Bring to a boil and lower heat. Simmer gently for 5 minutes. Add the potato to the pan along with the remaining stock. Bring to a boil, cover, and cook for 5 minutes. Add the vegetables, beans, and tomatoes. Bring mixture to a boil. Add pasta. Cook until pasta is tender, about 10 minutes. Serve with cheese on the side.

■ ■ ■

Three-Bean Vegetarian Chili

SERVES 6

Hearty, healthful, and satisfying, this chili is great over rice, couscous, or quinoa, or served with slices of whole-grain bread. Try adding a small amount of tomato paste for a stronger tomato flavor, or more beans for extra thickness.

2 Tbs. olive oil

2 medium onions, diced

2 small green bell peppers, diced

1 clove garlic, minced

2 cups cooked kidney beans,
  drained and rinsed if canned

2 cups cooked cannellini beans,
  drained and rinsed if canned

2 cups cooked black beans,
  drained and rinsed if canned

4 cups crushed tomatoes

2 cups diced tomatoes

1/2 tsp. dried basil or 1 1/2 tsp.
  minced fresh basil

1/4 tsp. cumin

1 Tbs. chili powder

2 cups cooked corn kernels

Heat oil in a medium stockpot over medium heat. Add onions, peppers, and garlic, and sauté for 5 minutes. Add beans, tomatoes, basil (if using dried), and spices, and simmer gently for 20 minutes. Add corn and fresh basil, and bring up to serving temperature.

Italian Skillet Mushroom Stew SERVES 4

Portabella mushrooms offer a "meaty" consistency to this low-fat vegetarian stew. You can replace or supplement them with cubed chicken breast or lean ground beef or turkey, if you desire. Use any pasta shape and size similar to elbow macaroni, such as shells, gnocchi, or spirals. For variation, replace the pasta with rice or couscous, which can be added directly to the skillet along with an extra cup of water or stock.

1/2 lb. medium pasta

1 Tbs. olive oil

8 oz. portabella mushrooms, cut into 1/2-inch cubes

12 to 16 oz. white button mushrooms, quartered

1 medium onion, chopped

1 cup diced celery

1 clove garlic, minced

4 cups crushed or diced tomatoes

1/2 lb. fresh green beans, cut in 2-inch pieces

1 tsp. dried basil or 1 Tbs. minced fresh basil

1/2 tsp. dried oregano or 1 1/2 tsp. minced fresh oregano

1/2 tsp. dried thyme or 1 1/2 tsp. fresh thyme

Salt and freshly ground black pepper, to taste

Cook pasta in plenty of boiling water until slightly underdone.

While pasta is cooking, heat the oil in a large nonstick skillet over medium heat. Add mushrooms, onion, celery, and garlic. Cook, stirring frequently, for 5 minutes. Add tomatoes, green beans, herbs, and salt and pepper to taste. Mix well, cover, and simmer for 10 minutes. Drain pasta and add to the skillet. Heat gently until pasta is done. Mix well and serve.

Spicy African Stew

SERVES 6

Choose your favorite thick and chunky salsa in a spiciness that appeals to you and your family, then add rice, vegetables, garbanzos, and peanut butter to create the flavors of Africa in a hearty, good-for-you stew.

1 Tbs. canola oil

1 medium onion, chopped

1 medium sweet potato, peeled and diced

2 cloves garlic, minced

1 small zucchini, peeled and diced

6 cups vegetable stock

¾ tsp. dried thyme or scant Tbs. fresh thyme

½ tsp. cumin powder

¾ cup long-grain white rice

16 oz. thick and chunky salsa

4 cups cooked garbanzo beans, drained and rinsed if canned

⅓ cup creamy peanut butter

In a large saucepan, heat the oil to medium high and sauté the onion, sweet potato, garlic, and zucchini about 5 minutes. Add the stock, thyme, cumin, and rice. Bring to a boil, reduce heat, cover, and simmer for 15 minutes. Add the salsa and beans, and bring to a boil. Add the peanut butter, and stir until combined. Serve hot.

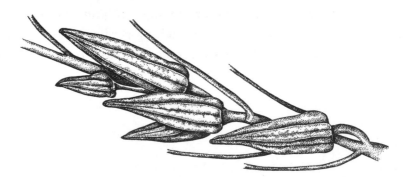

Caribbean Stew SERVES 6

This richly flavored vegetable stew gets its Caribbean essence from lime juice, hot pepper flakes, gingerroot, and cilantro. Combining sweet potatoes, cabbage, tomatoes, and okra gives a variety of textures and tastes. Serve over white or brown rice.

1 cup long-grain white rice or 4 servings instant brown rice, cooked according to package directions

2 Tbs. olive oil

2 cups chopped onion

3 cups chopped cabbage

¼ tsp. hot red pepper flakes

2 sweet potatoes, peeled and cut into ¾-inch cubes

1 Tbs. grated fresh gingerroot

2 cups water

4 cups diced tomato

2 cups sliced okra

3 Tbs. lime juice

2 Tbs. minced cilantro

Chopped peanuts (optional)

In a medium saucepan, combine the white rice and 2 cups of water; bring to a boil. Reduce the heat, cover, and simmer for 20 minutes or until all the liquid is absorbed. Keep the pan covered until ready to serve.

While rice is cooking, heat oil in a Dutch oven over medium heat. Add the onion, and sauté for 5 minutes. Add cabbage and red pepper flakes, and cook for 5 minutes, stirring often. Add sweet potatoes, gingerroot, and water, bring to a boil, and simmer, covered, for 5 minutes. Add tomatoes, okra, and lime juice. Cook 10 minutes, then stir in cilantro.

Serve over hot cooked rice, sprinkled with chopped peanuts, if desired.

Pasta Chowder

SERVES 4

If you like the smokiness of bacon in your chowder, sauté a small amount of bacon until it is completely crispy and remove it to drain on a paper towel; then crumble. Wipe out the pan and proceed with the recipe as written below. Add the cooked bacon with the vegetables.

1 tsp. olive oil

1 medium onion, diced

1 Tbs. all-purpose flour

5 cups skim milk

1/2 lb. ditalini, small shells, or other small pasta

1 medium potato, scrubbed or peeled, and diced

2 cups cooked corn kernels

1/2 tsp. dried thyme or 1 1/2 tsp. fresh thyme

1/2 tsp. crushed dried or minced fresh rosemary

Salt and freshly ground black pepper, to taste

Warm the oil in a large, nonstick Dutch oven over medium heat. Add the onion, and sauté for 5 minutes. Stir in the flour, then gradually whisk in the milk. Bring to a simmer, whisking constantly. Add the pasta and potato, and simmer slowly for 7 minutes. Stir in the corn and herbs, and simmer for 5 minutes more. Test pasta for doneness. Season to taste with salt and pepper before serving.

chicken

Chicken Pozole

SERVES 4

Pozole, or posole, *is the Mexican term for whole hominy, not to be confused with hominy grits. Hominy is dried white or yellow corn that has been cooked in water and lime until the skins can be slipped off easily. The kernels are then cooked in fresh water until they are tender and "bloom" or open up like a flower. The resulting product has the shape and consistency of a cooked garbanzo bean and the nutrition of corn. Pozole is available dried or canned.*

1 Tbs. olive oil

1 small onion, chopped

3/4 lb. skinless, boneless chicken breast, cut into small cubes

1 clove garlic, minced

1 tsp. dried oregano or 1 Tbs. minced fresh oregano

1 tsp. chili powder

3½ cups low-sodium chicken stock

2 cups cooked yellow or white pozole, drained and rinsed if canned

2 cups cooked black beans, drained and rinsed if canned

1 cup shredded cabbage

Corn tortillas

Heat the oil in a large saucepan or Dutch oven over medium heat. Add the onion, and cook for 5 minutes. Add chicken and garlic, and cook, stirring, for 3 minutes. Stir in the oregano and chili powder, and mix well. Add the stock, pozole, and beans, bring to a simmer, and cook until chicken pieces have lost their pink centers, about 5 minutes. Stir in the shredded cabbage, cook for 5 minutes, and serve with warm tortillas on the side.

Chicken and White Bean Stew SERVES 4

This hearty stew is thick with tender chicken breast chunks, tasty white beans, and potatoes. Its flavor comes from a combination of herbs, onion, and garlic, with no added fat or oil.

4 cups low-sodium chicken stock

1 small onion, minced

2 cloves garlic, minced

1 large baking potato, peeled and diced

1/2 lb. boneless, skinless chicken breast, cut into 3/4-inch cubes

2 cups cooked great northern, navy, or cannellini beans, drained and rinsed if canned

1/2 tsp. dried thyme or 1 1/2 tsp. fresh thyme

1/4 tsp. crushed dried or minced fresh rosemary

Salt and freshly ground black or white pepper, to taste

In a large saucepan, simmer minced onion and garlic in 1/2 cup of the stock for 5 minutes. Add the remainder of the stock and the potato pieces. Cover and bring to a boil, reduce heat, and simmer for 10 minutes. Remove approximately half the potatoes and 1 cup of stock, and set aside to cool.

Add chicken, beans, and herbs to remaining soup in pot. Bring to a boil, reduce heat, and simmer for 10 minutes.

While pot is simmering, purée reserved potatoes in their broth in a food processor or blender, or mash them with a potato masher. Return to the pot. Mix well and taste for seasoning. Add salt and pepper to taste, mix well, and serve.

Chicken and Rice Stew

SERVES 4

By adding more chicken stock, you can turn this satisfying one-dish meal into a body-warming soup. Boneless chicken thighs give a richer flavor than chicken breasts, with a minimum amount of extra fat. When using the chicken thighs, cook whole, then dice. If substituting breast, cut the meat into bite-sized cubes before cooking.

4 cups low-sodium chicken stock

¾ lb. boneless, skinless chicken thighs or breast

¾ cup long-grain white rice

5 cloves garlic, minced

1 bunch scallions, thinly sliced

2 cups cooked corn, green beans, peas, or a mixture of all three

2 Tbs. fresh lemon juice

1 tsp. dried or 1 Tbs. fresh dill weed

Salt and freshly ground black pepper, to taste

Combine the stock and chicken in a large saucepan. Cover and bring to a boil, reduce heat, and simmer, until chicken is cooked through, about 15 minutes for thighs, 5 to 8 minutes for chicken breast cubes.

If using thighs, remove them from the stock with a slotted spoon and return the stock to a boil. Add the rice, garlic, scallions, and vegetables. Reduce to a simmer, cover, and cook for 10 minutes. Dice the chicken thighs, and add them to the pot. Stir in the lemon juice and dill; cook 5 minutes longer. Season to taste with salt and pepper before serving.

Smoked Chicken Chowder

SERVES 4

Smoked chicken or turkey forms the flavorful base for a hearty chowder. Feel free to vary it with the addition of red peppers or mixed vegetables. The evaporated skim milk provides a creamy richness without the added fat from cream.

1 Tbs. olive oil

1 medium onion, minced

8 oz. mushrooms, sliced

1 small potato, peeled and cut into 1/4-inch cubes

1 clove garlic, minced

2 cups low-sodium chicken stock

1 cup cooked corn kernels

1/2 lb. smoked chicken breast, cut into 1/2-inch cubes

1 tsp. dried thyme or 1 Tbs. fresh thyme

3 Tbs. chopped fresh Italian parsley

10 oz. evaporated skim milk

Salt and freshly ground black pepper, to taste

1/2 cup shredded low-fat Monterey Jack cheese (about 2 oz.)

Heat the oil in a heavy saucepan over medium heat. Add the onion and mushrooms, and cook, stirring occasionally, for 5 minutes. Add potato and garlic, and cook, stirring, for 1 minute. Add stock, corn, chicken, and herbs, and bring to a boil. Lower heat, cover, and simmer, stirring occasionally, for 15 minutes, or until vegetables are tender. Add evaporated skim milk, season with salt and pepper, and warm through but do not boil. Stir in cheese, and serve hot.

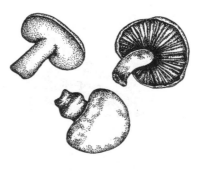

Turkey

Turkey Quinoa Soup   SERVES 4

Quinoa, grain of the Incas, is an ancient food native to the Americas that is regaining popularity due to its high nutritional profile. Quinoa is quick to cook and can be used in place of rice, couscous, millet, or other grains. Be sure to rinse it before cooking to remove a natural coating that can be bitter. Combined with other natives such as turkey, peppers, corn, and beans, quinoa contributes to a hearty soup.

1 Tbs. olive oil

1 medium onion, chopped

1 celery stalk, chopped

1 green bell pepper, chopped

4 cups low-sodium chicken stock

2 cups water

1/2 cup quinoa, rinsed well and drained

1 cup cooked corn

1 cup cooked cut green beans

1/2 lb. cooked turkey breast, sliced thick, cut into 1/2-inch chunks

Salt and freshly ground black pepper, to taste

Heat the oil in a large saucepan over medium heat. Add the onion, celery, and pepper, and cook until translucent, about 5 minutes. Add the stock and water, and bring to a boil. Stir in the quinoa, return to a boil, reduce heat, cover, and cook for 10 minutes. Add the corn, green beans, and turkey. Cook, covered, for 10 minutes. Season to taste and serve.

Ham

Potato, Ham, and Garlic Soup

This recipe can take advantage of leftover ham or be used with baked ham from the deli. Or, leave out the meat and use vegetable stock for a meatless meal. The addition of white beans is optional, but if you leave out the ham, be sure to add the beans.

6 cups low-sodium chicken or vegetable stock

2 cups diced, peeled potatoes

1 Tbs. olive oil

1 small onion, minced

1 small carrot, diced

4 cloves garlic, minced

4 oz. baked ham, cut into ½-inch cubes

2 cups cooked great northern or navy beans, drained and rinsed if canned (optional)

Salt and freshly ground black pepper, to taste

Bring the stock to a boil in a large saucepan or Dutch oven. Add the potatoes, cover, and return to a boil. Lower the heat, and simmer for 15 minutes.

Meanwhile, heat the oil in a medium nonstick skillet over medium heat. Add the onion and carrot, and cook, stirring occasionally, for 5 minutes. Add the garlic, mix well, and cook 2 minutes. Add the ham, remove from the heat, cover, and keep warm.

With a slotted spoon, transfer approximately half of the cooked potatoes to a food processor or blender, along with 1 cup of the hot stock. Purée until smooth. Return the puréed potatoes to the soup, and stir in the ham mixture. Stir in the beans. Cover and simmer for 5 minutes. Season to taste with salt and pepper before serving.

Beef

Black Bean Chili

SERVES 5 (NO MEAT) OR 6 (WITH MEAT)

This tomato-less chili lends itself to a range of variations, and can be served over any grain-based product such as orzo, quinoa, or barley. But whatever you do, don't leave out the prunes. They add a satisfying sweetness and richness, and help you meet your family's daily need for five servings of fruits and vegetables.

1 cup long-grain white rice or 4 servings instant brown rice, cooked according to package directions

1 lb. lean ground turkey or beef (optional)

1 tsp. olive oil

1 medium onion, finely chopped

3 cloves garlic, chopped

2 Tbs. chili powder

2¼ cups water

12 whole pitted prunes (about ¼ lb.), chopped

2 cups cooked black beans, drained and rinsed if canned, or 4 cups if not using meat

In a medium saucepan, combine the white rice and 2 cups of water; bring to a boil. Reduce the heat, cover, and simmer for 20 minutes or until all the liquid is absorbed. Keep the pan covered until ready to serve.

Cook ground meat in a large nonstick skillet over medium-high heat until browned, stirring to break into crumbles. Remove to a colander and rinse with hot water, then drain well. Wipe out skillet, then heat oil in skillet and add onion and garlic. Sauté for 5 minutes. Add chili powder, and cook 1 minute. Return meat to skillet and stir in water, prunes, and beans. Bring to a boil, reduce heat, and simmer, uncovered, 5 minutes. Serve over rice.

Chipotle Chili   SERVES 4 TO 6

*Chipotle peppers are smoke-dried jalapeño peppers with a unique flavor,
available in dried form or canned in a tomato (adobo) sauce. Lean ground
beef or turkey is optional; replace with extra beans for a meatless meal,
using a mixture of pinto and red kidney for interest and color.*

8 oz. ditalini, small shells, or other small pasta

2 tsp. plus 1 Tbs. olive oil, divided

6 oz. lean ground beef or ground turkey (optional)

1 medium onion, chopped

3 cloves garlic, minced

2 chipotle peppers canned in *adobo* sauce, minced

2 tsp. ground cumin

1/2 tsp. dried oregano or 1 1/2 tsp. minced fresh oregano

4 cups diced tomato

2 cups cooked pinto or red kidney beans, rinsed and drained if canned, or 4 cups if not using meat

1/4 cup chopped cilantro

Cook pasta in plenty of boiling water until done but still firm to the bite
(al dente). Drain pasta, reserving 2 cups of pasta water.

While the pasta cooks, heat the 2 teaspoons of oil in a large nonstick skillet over medium-high heat. Add the ground meat, and cook
until browned, stirring often to break into crumbles. Remove to a colander to drain away excess fat; rinse with hot water. Wipe out the skillet
and heat the tablespoon of oil over medium heat. Add the onion and
garlic, and cook for 3 minutes. Add the chipotles, and cook, stirring,
until they break up. Return the cooked meat to the pan and add the
cumin, oregano, tomatoes, and beans, mixing well. Bring to a boil,
reduce heat and simmer, uncovered, for 5 minutes. Stir in cilantro, and
simmer for 2 minutes more. Add pasta to chili and adjust liquid as
needed with pasta water before serving.

Hot Dishes

vegetarian

Company Rice   SERVES 6

Vary the vegetables and beans for innumerable combinations to give this dish a new personality each time you serve it. Cooked, cubed pieces of chicken, turkey, pork, bacon, or crumbled ground beef can be stirred in with, or in place of, the beans.

1 cup long-grain white rice or 4 servings instant brown rice, cooked according to package directions

1 Tbs. olive oil

1 medium onion, coarsely chopped

2 cloves garlic, finely minced

1/2 lb. mushrooms, sliced

2 cups diced tomatoes

1 medium zucchini (about 1/2 lb.), coarsely chopped

1/2 tsp. dried oregano or 1 1/2 tsp. minced fresh oregano

2 cups cooked kidney, pink, black, or garbanzo beans, drained and rinsed if canned

Salt and freshly ground black pepper, to taste

1 cup shredded low-fat cheddar or Monterey Jack cheese

In a medium saucepan, combine the white rice and 2 cups of water; bring to a boil. Reduce the heat, cover, and simmer for 20 minutes or until all the liquid is absorbed. Keep the pan covered until ready to serve.

While the rice is cooking, heat the oil in a large nonstick skillet over medium heat. Add the onion and garlic, and sauté for 5 minutes. Add the mushrooms, and sauté 5 minutes more. Add the tomatoes, zucchini, and oregano. Cover the skillet, and simmer the mixture for about 5 minutes. Add the beans to the pan. Simmer the mixture, stirring it occasionally, until it is heated through. Season to taste with salt and pepper.

To serve, spoon the vegetable-bean mixture over the hot rice, and sprinkle the cheese on top.

Mexicali Beans and Rice

SERVES 4

Use fresh, ripe tomatoes in season, and vary the recipe with the addition of diced, cooked meat if you wish. If you double the recipe, use two types of beans for interest.

1 cup long-grain white rice or 4 servings instant brown rice, cooked according to package directions

1 Tbs. olive oil

1 medium onion, coarsely chopped

2 cloves garlic, finely minced

1/2 lb. mushrooms, sliced (optional)

2 red, yellow, or orange bell peppers, chopped

2 cups diced tomatoes

8 oz. salsa or picante sauce

1/2 tsp. dried oregano or 1 1/2 tsp. minced fresh oregano

2 cups cooked aduki, black, or pinto beans, drained and rinsed if canned

1 1/2 tsp. chili powder, or more to taste

1 cup shredded low-fat Monterey Jack, mozzarella, or cheddar cheese

In a medium saucepan, combine the white rice and 2 cups of water; bring to a boil. Reduce the heat, cover, and simmer for 20 minutes or until all the liquid is absorbed. Keep the pan covered until ready to serve.

While the rice is cooking, heat the oil in a large nonstick skillet over medium heat. Add the onion and garlic, and sauté for 5 minutes. Add the mushrooms and peppers, and sauté 5 minutes more. Add the tomatoes, salsa, and oregano. Cover the skillet, and simmer the mixture for about 5 minutes. Add the beans to the pan. Simmer the mixture, stirring it occasionally, until it is heated through. Season to taste with chili powder, mixing well.

To serve, gently stir in cooked rice, and sprinkle the cheese on top.

Middle Eastern Skillet

SERVES 4

Be sure to use baby or Japanese eggplant to avoid the need to salt the egg-plant to remove bitterness. If you prefer, you can replace the eggplant in this recipe with broccoli, zucchini, or summer squash.

1 cup couscous, rice, or millet

2 Tbs. olive oil

1 medium onion, chopped

1 green bell pepper, diced

1 small eggplant, cubed

2 cloves garlic, minced

1 tsp. cumin

1 tsp. dried basil or 1 Tbs. minced fresh basil

2 cups cooked garbanzo beans, rinsed and drained if canned

SAUCE:

2 Tbs. lemon juice

3 Tbs. tahini

1/4 cup nonfat plain yogurt

2 Tbs. tamari, or to taste

1/2 cup chopped fresh Italian parsley

If using couscous, place 1 cup of couscous in a large bowl, and add 1¼ cups boiling water. Cover and allow to sit for 5 minutes or until the water is absorbed. If cooking rice or millet, combine 1 cup of grain with 2 cups of water in a medium saucepan, and bring to a boil. Reduce the heat, cover, and simmer for 20 minutes or until all the liquid is absorbed. Keep the pan covered until ready to serve.

Heat the oil in a large nonstick skillet over medium heat. Add the onion and pepper, and sauté for 3 minutes. Add eggplant, garlic, cumin, and basil (if using dried). Stir over high heat for 2 minutes. Lower the heat, cover, and cook until the eggplant is tender, stirring occasionally. Add the garbanzo beans and fresh basil, and heat through over medium heat.

In a small bowl, mix together sauce ingredients. Remove the skillet from the heat and stir in the sauce. Warm over low heat, but do not continue to cook. Serve immediately over cooked couscous, rice, or millet.

Miami Rice

SERVES 6

A classic combination of beans and rice, this dish takes its flavor from cumin, oregano, and hot pepper sauce. Adding orange juice to canned tomatoes "refreshes" their just-picked taste.

1½ cups long-grain white rice or 6 servings of instant brown rice, cooked according to package directions

1 Tbs. olive oil

1 large onion, diced

1 green bell pepper, chopped

1 red bell pepper, chopped

3 large cloves garlic, minced

1 Tbs. ground cumin

1 tsp. dried oregano or 1 Tbs. minced fresh oregano

4 cups cooked black beans, drained and rinsed if canned

2 cups diced tomatoes

¼ cup orange juice

1 tsp. hot pepper sauce

In a medium saucepan, combine the white rice and 3 cups of water; bring to a boil. Reduce the heat, cover, and simmer for 20 minutes or until all the liquid is absorbed. Keep the pan covered until ready to serve.

While rice is cooking, heat oil in a large nonstick skillet over medium heat. Add onion, bell peppers, garlic, cumin, and oregano (if using dried). Sauté until vegetables are tender, about 5 minutes. Mash ½ cup of the beans. Add mashed beans, whole beans, tomatoes, orange juice, and hot pepper sauce. Bring to a boil, stirring frequently. Reduce heat and simmer, uncovered, for 15 minutes. Add fresh oregano, mix, and serve over hot cooked rice.

Portabella Cassoulet   SERVES 4

This vegetarian version of the French classic uses portabella mushrooms as its source of rich flavor and meaty texture. Serve with a green salad and plenty of good French bread.

8 oz. portabella mushrooms, sliced ½-inch thick

3 Tbs. olive oil

3 large cloves garlic, chopped

2 cups diced tomatoes

1 tsp. dried thyme or 1 Tbs. fresh thyme

2 tsp. dried basil or 2 Tbs. minced fresh basil

1 tsp. crushed dried or minced fresh rosemary

1 bay leaf

½ lb. small to medium onions, quartered

Salt and freshly ground black pepper, to taste

4 cups cooked navy or great northern beans, drained and rinsed if canned

Lightly brush cut sides of mushroom slices with 1 tablespoon of the olive oil. Heat a large heavy skillet or casserole over medium heat, and sauté the mushrooms for 1 to 2 minutes on each side. Mushrooms should brown, but remain soft. Remove from the heat and let cool. Cut into bite-sized pieces and set aside.

Return the skillet to the heat and warm the remaining 2 tablespoons of oil. Add garlic, and sauté for 30 seconds. Do not allow the garlic to brown. Add tomatoes, and cook 1 minute over high heat. Add mushrooms, herbs (if using dried), and bay leaf. Stir and bring to a boil. Add onions and salt and pepper to taste. Return to a boil, cover, and simmer over low heat for 15 minutes, stirring occasionally. Remove and discard the bay leaf. Mix in the beans and fresh herbs, and simmer over low to medium heat until beans are warmed through, about 5 minutes. Add water, if necessary, to keep ingredients moist. Adjust seasonings and serve.

Grampa's Saturday Night Kale

SERVES 6

My Sicilian grandfather harvested the kale for this dish directly from his large urban garden. For authentic flavor, use lacinata kale (Cavolo nero), if you can find it. If you prefer, replace vitamin-rich kale with any deep-colored leafy green such as spinach or chard. Choose a pasta with substance, such as rotini, gemelli, or penne.

12 ounces kale, spinach, or chard

1 lb. medium-sized pasta

1/4 cup olive oil

4 large cloves garlic, minced

2 cups diced tomatoes

1/4 tsp. hot red pepper flakes

2 cups cooked garbanzo beans, drained and rinsed if canned

Salt, to taste

3/4 cup freshly grated Romano cheese

Bring a large pot of water to a boil. Wash kale, remove center ribs, and cut into bite-sized strips. Add kale to pot and cook for 3 to 5 minutes, until leaves wilt and soften. Remove kale from the water and set aside. Return the water to a boil and add the pasta. Cook until done, but still firm to the bite (al dente). Reserve 1/2 cup of the cooking water before draining the pasta.

While pasta is cooking, heat oil in a large nonstick skillet over moderate heat. Add the garlic, and sauté for 1 minute. Add the tomatoes, red pepper flakes, and garbanzos. Simmer gently for 10 minutes. Season with salt to taste. Stir in cooked kale.

Place pasta in a large bowl and add the contents of the skillet. Gently stir in the cheese. Add reserved pasta water as needed to keep the dish moist. Serve immediately.

Monterey Couscous

SERVES 6

Citrus flavors add interest to this quick meal that takes advantage of the five-minute preparation time of couscous.

3¼ cups vegetable stock	¼ cup orange juice
1½ cups couscous	¼ cup lemon juice
1 small red bell pepper, diced	1 Tbs. olive oil
1 cup cooked or frozen corn kernels	¼ tsp. ground cumin
2 cups cooked black or pinto beans, drained and rinsed if canned	Salt and freshly ground black pepper, to taste

Bring the stock to a boil in a saucepan. Place the couscous in a bowl, and add 2¼ cups of the boiling stock. Cover and let sit for 5 minutes or until all of the liquid is absorbed.

Place the pepper, corn, and beans in the remaining stock, and bring to a boil. Reduce heat, cover, and simmer for 10 minutes. Add the juices, oil, and cumin, and salt and pepper to taste. Bring to a boil.

Fluff the couscous with a fork, pour the sauce over the couscous, mix well, and serve.

Burgundy Lentils

If you are making this dish for adults and would like to increase its richness and classic French taste, use a total of 2 cups of dry red wine (Burgundy is traditional) in place of the stock and wine listed below. If you wish to leave out all alcohol, try a nonalcoholic red wine or replace the wine with an additional ½ cup of stock.

2 Tbs. olive oil

1 large onion, chopped

2 cloves garlic, minced

½ lb. mushrooms, sliced

½ cup dry red wine

1 large potato, peeled and cubed

1 large carrot, sliced lengthwise and then in thin half-coins

1½ cups lentils, preferably French green, picked over and rinsed

2 cups water

1½ cups vegetable stock

3 Tbs. tomato paste

1 tsp. dried thyme or 1 Tbs. fresh thyme

2 bay leaves

1 Tbs. balsamic or red wine vinegar

Salt and freshly ground black pepper, to taste

Heat the olive oil in a heavy stock pot over medium heat. Add the onion, garlic, and mushrooms, and sauté for 5 minutes. Add the wine and cook for 2 minutes. Add the remaining ingredients, except salt and pepper, and bring to a boil. Reduce heat, cover, and simmer until potatoes, carrots, and lentils are cooked, about 20 minutes. Add more water or stock, if necessary, to keep vegetables and lentils almost covered. Remove bay leaves, taste for seasonings, adjust with salt and pepper, and serve.

Dixie Pasta and Greens SERVES 6

Depending upon what's in season, use this recipe with kale, chicory, mustard greens, or any other green. Black-eyed peas can be replaced with navy or great northern beans. Season to taste with hot pepper sauce, and you have a taste of the South.

6 oz. radiatore or other medium pasta

2 tsp. olive oil

1 green bell pepper, chopped

1 small onion, chopped

1 celery stalk, chopped

1 clove garlic, minced

2 cups water or vegetable stock

2 Tbs. tomato paste

1 tsp. dried oregano or 1 Tbs. chopped fresh oregano

Freshly ground black pepper, to taste

1 cup cooked black-eyed peas

1 bunch kale, mustard greens, or chicory

2 to 3 drops hot pepper sauce

Cook pasta in plenty of boiling water until done but still firm to the bite (al dente).

While pasta cooks, heat olive oil in a large saucepan over medium heat. Add the pepper, onion, celery, and garlic, and cook for 3 minutes. Add water or stock, tomato paste, oregano (if using dried), and black pepper. Bring to a boil. Stir in black-eyed peas, cover, and simmer over low heat 15 minutes.

Chop greens, and add to saucepan. Cover, and cook for 3 minutes. Stir in fresh oregano and the drained pasta. Cook until heated through. Season to taste with hot pepper sauce, and serve.

Spinach and Bean Bowties   SERVES 6

Sharp Italian or Greek cheese adds flavor to this simple, tomato-less pasta dish that is high in nutrition. Use a crumbly cheese such as ricotta salata or feta, and if you are not intent on keeping it vegetarian, replace the vegetable stock with low-sodium, low-fat chicken stock.

12 ounces bowtie pasta

1 Tbs. olive oil

1 Spanish onion, thinly sliced

2 cloves garlic, minced

3/4 cup vegetable stock

1/4 tsp. hot red pepper flakes

2 cups cannellini beans, drained and rinsed if canned

Salt and freshly ground black pepper, to taste

1 lb. fresh spinach, washed and coarsely chopped

2 oz. ricotta salata or feta cheese, crumbled

Cook pasta in plenty of boiling water until done but still firm to the bite (al dente).

While pasta cooks, heat olive oil in a large nonstick skillet over medium heat. Add the onion and garlic, and cook for 5 minutes. Add the stock, hot red pepper flakes, and beans, and season with salt and pepper. Cook over medium-high heat until the beans are heated through, about 5 minutes.

Just before pasta is done, add the spinach to the water, and stir until spinach wilts. Drain pasta and spinach, and put in a serving bowl. Add the sauce, and toss to mix well. Add the cheese, mix lightly, and serve.

Asian Spicy Rice

SERVES 6

This dish can be served at room temperature, cold, or hot, and makes a complete vegetarian meal or a tasty side dish. For an even heartier meal, add cooked shrimp or chicken.

1 cup aromatic white rice
(jasmine, Texmati, or basmati)

¼ cup silken tofu

⅓ cup smooth peanut butter

2 Tbs. rice vinegar (unseasoned)
or white wine vinegar

1 Tbs. tamari

2 tsp. lime juice

1 tsp. toasted sesame oil

1 clove garlic

¼ tsp. hot red pepper flakes

½ cup chopped cilantro

4 scallions, thinly sliced

In a medium saucepan, combine the white rice and 2 cups of water; bring to a boil. Reduce the heat, cover, and simmer for 20 minutes or until all the liquid is absorbed. Let sit off heat for 10 minutes, then fluff with a fork. Keep the pan covered until ready to serve.

In a blender or food processor, combine the tofu, peanut butter, vinegar, tamari, lime juice, sesame oil, garlic, and red pepper flakes. Purée until smooth. Stir in the cilantro and scallions. Add the rice, mix well, and serve.

Colored Pepper Pasta

SERVES 4

This quick and easy pasta dish is high in vitamin C from the fresh bell peppers and tomato salsa. Balsamic vinegar adds a mellow, lightly sweet and tangy touch to this richly flavored dish.

12 oz. ziti, penne, or other medium pasta

2 Tbs. olive oil

1 large onion, chopped

1 green bell pepper, cut into short thin strips

1 red bell pepper, cut into short thin strips

1 yellow bell pepper, cut into short thin strips

1 Tbs. minced garlic

1 tsp. dried basil or 1 Tbs. minced fresh basil

1/2 tsp. dried oregano or 1 1/2 tsp. minced fresh oregano

8 oz. prepared salsa

2 Tbs. balsamic vinegar

1/4 cup grated Parmesan cheese

Cook pasta in plenty of boiling water until done but still firm to the bite (al dente).

While pasta is cooking, heat oil in a large nonstick skillet over medium heat. Cook onion, peppers, garlic, and herbs (if using dried), stirring frequently, for 5 minutes. Add salsa, fresh herbs, and vinegar. Stir well, and cook for 2 minutes. Drain pasta, top with pepper mixture and cheese. Toss well before serving, with additional cheese, if desired.

Spicy Vegetable Couscous

SERVES 6

Couscous is a precooked form of semolina pasta that takes only 5 minutes to prepare. It comes in both whole wheat and refined wheat forms; the cooking time is the same for both. For a change of pace and nutrition, use couscous wherever you would use rice.

1 cup couscous

3 cups vegetable stock or water, divided

1 Tbs. olive oil

1 medium onion, finely chopped

4 cloves garlic, minced

1 Tbs. finely chopped fresh gingerroot

4 carrots, cut into coins

Pinch hot red pepper flakes

1/8 tsp. ground coriander

2 zucchini, cut into 1/2-inch rounds

1 red bell pepper, cut into 1/2-inch pieces

Put the couscous in a large bowl and add 1 cup of boiling stock or water. Cover the bowl and let stand for 5 minutes.

Heat the oil in a large nonstick skillet over medium heat. Add the onions, garlic, and ginger, and cook, stirring, for 1 minute. Add the carrots, red pepper flakes, coriander, and remaining stock. Bring to a boil, reduce heat, cover, and cook for 5 minutes. Add the zucchini, cover, and cook for 3 minutes. Add the red bell pepper, and cook, uncovered, for 3 minutes.

Fluff the couscous with a fork. Pour the vegetables and cooking liquid over it, mix, and serve.

Creamy Ziti

SERVES 6

This dish makes use of the blender or food processor to purée vegetables and other ingredients into a creamy sauce that can be tossed with ziti, penne, or other medium pasta shapes. Vary the vegetables that are left whole, or stir cooked chicken, turkey, or ham into sauce before heating it.

12 oz. ziti, penne, or other medium pasta

1/2 tsp. olive oil

1 small onion, diced

1 red bell pepper, diced

1 yellow bell pepper, diced

1 cup nonfat sour cream

1/2 lb. fresh spinach, washed and dried

3/4 cup skim milk

1/4 cup Dijon-style mustard

3 Tbs. minced fresh Italian parsley

1 tsp. dried dill leaves or 1 Tbs. minced fresh dill leaves

1 Tbs. lemon juice

3/4 tsp. hot pepper sauce

Cook pasta in plenty of boiling water until done but still firm to the bite (al dente).

While pasta is cooking, warm the oil in a large nonstick skillet over medium heat. Add the onion and the red and yellow bell peppers, cover the pan, and cook for 5 minutes or until peppers are soft.

Purée the sour cream, spinach, milk, mustard, parsley, dill, lemon juice, and hot pepper sauce in a food processor or blender until very smooth. Add to the vegetables in the skillet and heat to a simmer.

Drain pasta well and toss with the sauce. Season to taste with salt and pepper.

Fettucine with
Three-Mushroom Sauté
SERVES 4

Use either fresh or dried fettucine for this dish, and if you want to make "Hay and Straw," mix plain and spinach pastas together. Feel free to substitute mushroom varieties as available, but do use some wild, as they add a unique European flavor to the dish.

12 oz. dry or 16 oz. fresh plain or spinach fettucine

1 Tbs. pine nuts

1 Tbs. olive oil

8 oz. button mushrooms, coarsely chopped

4 oz. shiitake mushrooms, stems discarded, caps coarsely chopped

4 oz. cremini, oyster, or cepe mushrooms, coarsely chopped

1 can artichoke hearts, drained and chopped

1 cup vegetable stock

1 Tbs. cornstarch

1/2 cup evaporated skim milk

12 spinach leaves, coarse stems removed, leaves thinly sliced

1/2 cup crumbled feta cheese

Freshly ground black pepper, to taste

Cook pasta in plenty of boiling water until done but still firm to the bite (al dente).

While pasta is cooking, toast the pine nuts in a dry skillet for 5 minutes or until golden brown. Chop the nuts and set them aside.

Heat the oil in a large, nonstick skillet over medium heat. Add the mushrooms, and sauté until soft, about 5 minutes. Add the artichoke hearts and the stock, and bring to a simmer. In a small bowl, whisk together the evaporated milk and cornstarch; stir milk mixture into the mushrooms. Simmer for 2 minutes.

Toss the sauce with the pasta, spinach, and feta cheese. Season with pepper, sprinkle with pine nuts, and serve.

Pasta Primavera   SERVES 4

This primavera is loaded with fresh, in-season vegetables and herbs and enhanced with the richness of sun-dried tomatoes. The ingredient list is long, but the preparation is a quick stir-fry that puts this summertime supper together in no time.

8 oz. rotini, twists, or spirals
1 Tbs. olive oil
2 cloves garlic, minced
Pinch of hot red pepper flakes
3 medium carrots, thinly sliced
1 medium red onion, sliced vertically
2 small zucchini, sliced
2 small yellow squash, sliced

½ lb. fresh green beans, cut into 1-inch pieces
¼ cup water
¼ cup chopped fresh basil
½ cup oil-packed sun-dried tomatoes, drained and chopped
Freshly grated Parmesan or Romano cheese

Cook pasta in plenty of boiling water until done but still firm to the bite (al dente).

While pasta is cooking, heat the oil in a large nonstick skillet over medium heat. Add the garlic and red pepper flakes, and cook for 1 minute. Add carrots, onion, zucchini, squash, and beans, and stir-fry for 5 minutes. Add water, bring to a boil, and simmer 1 minute. In a large serving bowl, toss together the pasta, vegetables, basil, and sun-dried tomatoes. Serve with grated cheese on the side.

Pasta with Tomato "Cream" SERVES 6

Using evaporated skim milk to replace cream gives this delicious vegetable pasta dish the flavor of a high-calorie cream sauce with the nutritional advantage of a low-fat dish. Add seasonal vegetables of your choice, such as green beans or broccoli, to personalize the recipe, and use fresh ripe tomatoes in season.

1 lb. penne, mostaccioli, or spiral pasta

1 Tbs. olive oil

1 medium carrot, cut into thin coins

2 red bell peppers, cut into thin strips

1 medium onion, thinly sliced

3 cloves garlic, minced

4 cups diced tomatoes

1 tsp. dried basil or 1 Tbs. minced fresh basil

Salt and freshly ground black pepper, to taste

4 tsp. flour

1/2 cup evaporated skim milk

Cook pasta in plenty of boiling water until done but still firm to the bite (al dente).

While pasta is cooking, warm the oil in a large nonstick skillet over medium-high heat. Gently sauté the carrot, peppers, onion, and garlic about 10 minutes. Stir in the tomatoes, basil (if using dried), and seasonings; cover and bring to a boil. Reduce heat and simmer for 10 minutes.

Combine flour and milk, and stir well. Slowly add milk mixture to the sauce, stirring constantly, until slightly thickened. Add fresh basil. Drain pasta well and add to skillet. Toss gently and serve.

Peanut Veggie Stir-Fry

SERVES 4

Peanut sauce and roasted peanuts give this quick dish an Asian flavor and an interesting crunch. Vary the stir-fry vegetables, using broccoli or cauliflower florets, cabbage, sugar snap peas, or other family favorites. Adjust stir-frying time accordingly. Use a fragrant long-grain white rice such as basmati or Texmati for texture and added flavor. If you wish to add meat, try 1/2 lb. of boneless, skinless chicken breast cut in strips.

1 cup long-grain white rice or 4 servings instant brown rice, cooked according to package directions

1 tsp. canola or peanut oil

1 medium onion, cut in short strips

1 medium carrot, cut julienne

1 green bell pepper, diced

4 oz. mushrooms, thinly sliced

1/2 lb. snow peas or snap peas

1/2 tsp. hot red pepper flakes

1/4 cup roasted, unsalted peanuts

SAUCE:

3 Tbs. smooth peanut butter

1/3 cup lime juice

1/4 cup tamari

1/4 cup water

In a medium saucepan, combine the white rice and 2 cups of water; bring to a boil. Reduce the heat, cover, and simmer for 20 minutes or until all the liquid is absorbed. Keep the pan covered until ready to serve.

While rice is cooking, heat a large wok or nonstick skillet over high heat. Add the oil to the pan and warm. Add the onion, carrot, and green bell pepper, and stir-fry for 2 to 3 minutes. Add the mushrooms, snow peas, and hot pepper flakes, and stir-fry for 2 minutes more. Add peanuts.

Mix sauce ingredients in a small bowl and add to wok or skillet. Stir gently and bring to a boil. Serve over rice.

Ratatouille Rice   SERVES 6

The classic ratatouille originated in southern France, where the word means "poor man's stew." Ratatouille is a vegetable stew; we are adding the dimension of rice to round out the meal. While ratatouille benefits from an opportunity to have its flavors meld over time, it still lends itself to a quick meal, and the leftovers will only get better! Serve hot, at room temperature, or chilled.

1 cup long-grain white rice or 4 servings instant brown rice, cooked according to package directions

3 Tbs. olive oil

1 medium onion, coarsely chopped

2 cloves garlic, finely minced

1/2 tsp. dried basil or 1 1/2 tsp. minced fresh basil

1/2 tsp. dried oregano or 1 1/2 tsp. minced fresh oregano

1/2 tsp. dried thyme or 1 1/2 tsp. fresh thyme

1/2 tsp. crumbled dried or minced fresh rosemary

2 lb. ripe tomatoes, peeled, seeded, and finely diced

1/4 tsp. freshly ground black pepper

2 medium zucchini or 1 each zucchini and yellow squash, sliced 1/4-inch thick

1 green bell pepper, thinly sliced

1 red bell pepper, thinly sliced

2 small or 1 medium eggplant, peeled and cubed

In a medium saucepan, combine the white rice and 2 cups of water; bring to a boil. Reduce the heat, cover, and simmer for 20 minutes or until all the liquid is absorbed. Keep the pan covered until ready to serve.

While rice is cooking, heat olive oil in a heavy pot over medium heat. Add onion, and sauté for 5 minutes. Add garlic and herbs (if using dried), and sauté briefly. Stir in tomatoes and black pepper. Bring to a boil. Add zucchini, green and red peppers, and eggplant. Cover and simmer gently for 20 minutes. Stir in fresh herbs, and serve over rice.

Pasta Siciliano

Sicilian cooking uses ingredients introduced to the island over the centuries by a number of other cultures, including Greek, North African, and Spanish. Capers, raisins, and almonds join tomatoes, basil, and garlic in this quick, uncooked sauce with added spice from hot red pepper flakes. Serve with a light salad and good Italian or French bread.

12 oz. spaghetti, linguine, or gemelli

2/3 cup blanched almonds

1 lb. ripe plum tomatoes, peeled and halved

2 cloves garlic, thinly sliced

1 cup lightly packed fresh basil leaves

Pinch hot red pepper flakes

1/4 cup extra-virgin olive oil

1 Tbs. capers, rinsed

2 Tbs. golden raisins

Cook pasta in plenty of boiling water until done but still firm to the bite (al dente).

While pasta is cooking, lightly toast the almonds in a dry frying pan over medium heat, stirring continuously. Set aside to cool.

In a food processor, combine the almonds, tomatoes, garlic, basil, and hot red pepper flakes. Process until well chopped, scraping down the sides as needed. With the motor running, add the oil through the feed tube until the mixture is well-blended but still coarse. It may not be necessary to use all of the oil. Transfer to a bowl, and mix in capers and golden raisins.

Drain pasta, reserving 1/2 cup of cooking water. Toss pasta with sauce, adding hot pasta cooking water as needed to achieve desired consistency.

Portabella Sauce with Orzo

SERVES 4

In its longer version, this recipe calls for the vegetables to be gently baked in an oven for an hour to blend their flavors and create a savory gravy. This quick stir-fry method does its best to re-create that, using the tamari for added richness. Rice, couscous, or quinoa would work equally well in place of the orzo, and the sauce would also be good over small shells or bowties.

8 oz. orzo

2 tsp. olive oil

1 medium onion, coarsely chopped

4 garlic cloves, smashed and coarsely chopped

2 medium yellow summer squash, cut into 1/2-inch cubes

1 medium zucchini, cut into 1/2-inch cubes

1 large portabella mushroom, cut into 1/2-inch cubes

2 cups diced tomatoes

1 tsp. dried thyme or 1 Tbs. fresh thyme

1 tsp. tamari

Freshly ground black pepper, to taste

2 Tbs. pine nuts

Cook orzo in plenty of boiling water until done but still firm to the bite (al dente).

While pasta is cooking, heat oil in a medium nonstick skillet or wok over medium heat. Add onion, and sauté until it softens but does not brown, 2 to 3 minutes. Add garlic and squash, and stir-fry for 2 to 3 minutes. Add mushroom, and stir-fry for 2 minutes longer. Stir in tomatoes, thyme, and tamari, and season to taste with pepper. Add pine nuts. Cover and simmer for 10 minutes to blend flavors. Serve over orzo.

■ ■ ■

Mushroom and Broccoli Bulgur

SERVES 4

Use a mixture of mushrooms, choosing from the many "wild" varieties on the shelves, including crimini, shiitake, oyster, enoki, or portabella, in addition to the widely used white, to enhance the flavor and vary the texture. If the price of wild varieties seems high, remember that this recipe contains no meat to drive up the cost. Experiment with other vegetables and/or grains to personalize this pilaf to meet your family's tastes, using quinoa, white or brown rice, or couscous, and adjusting the cooking times accordingly.

1 lb. sliced mushrooms, your choice of varieties

1 small onion, diced

2 large cloves garlic, minced

1¾ cups vegetable stock

1 cup bulgur

¾ lb. broccoli florets

Salt and freshly ground black pepper, to taste

Freshly grated Romano or Parmesan cheese

Sauté the mushrooms, onion, and garlic in 2 to 3 tablespoons of the stock until vegetables are tender, about 5 minutes. Add the remainder of the stock and bring to a boil. Add the bulgur and broccoli florets. Reduce heat and simmer, covered, until liquid is absorbed, about 15 minutes. Season with salt and pepper to taste. Serve with freshly grated cheese.

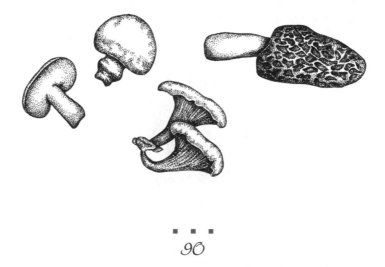

Veggie Pasta with Garlic Sauce SERVES 6

Vary the greens in this recipe each time you make it by using vegetables in season. Choose a smooth sweet potato to facilitate peeling. Diced cooked chicken could also be added, and would blend nicely with the garlic sauce.

12 oz. shells, rotini, gemelli, or other medium pasta

6 to 8 large garlic cloves, peeled and minced

3/4 cup vegetable stock

2 Tbs. olive oil

1 small sweet potato, peeled and diced into 1/2-inch pieces

2 small red potatoes, scrubbed and diced into 1/2-inch pieces

1/2 lb. green beans, cut into 2-inch lengths

1/2 lb. fresh shelled peas

In a small saucepan, combine the garlic and stock. Bring to a boil, reduce the heat to low, cover, and simmer until the garlic releases its fragrance, about 5 minutes. Remove from the heat, uncover, and let cool. Transfer the garlic and the stock to a food processor or blender and purée until smooth. Add the olive oil and purée until blended.

Bring a large pot of salted water to a boil and add the pasta. Cook for 3 minutes. Add the vegetables and cook for 10 minutes or until the pasta is al dente and the vegetables are tender.

Drain the pasta and vegetables, reserving 1/2 cup of the cooking water. Put the pasta and vegetables into a serving bowl, scrape the garlic purée over the pasta, and toss to mix, adding cooking water as needed to achieve appropriate consistency. Serve at once.

Pasta with Greens and Ricotta   SERVES 4

Use your favorite greens in this recipe, from arugula through watercress, and top with either toasted walnuts or pine nuts. Any pasta will do, from long narrow types such as fettucine to twists, bowties, or shells. Serve with crunchy French or Italian bread.

12 oz. pasta, any type

¼ cup pine nuts or walnuts

1 Tbs. olive oil

2 cloves garlic, minced

5 cups chopped spinach, Swiss chard, kale, arugula, watercress, or broccoli rabe

¼ cup water

Salt and freshly ground black pepper, to taste

¼ tsp. nutmeg

¾ cup part-skim ricotta cheese

Crumbled ricotta salata or grated Parmesan

1 large fresh tomato, peeled, seeded, and chopped

Cook pasta in plenty of boiling water until done but still firm to the bite (al dente).

While pasta is cooking, toast the nuts in a dry skillet until golden, and set aside. Heat the oil in a large nonstick skillet over medium heat. Add the garlic and sauté for 1 minute. Add the greens and water, and cook, stirring often, until the greens just begin to wilt. Season with salt, pepper, and nutmeg; mix well and transfer to a blender or food processor. Add the ricotta, and purée until smooth and evenly colored. Taste for seasoning and adjust. Stir in the ricotta salata. Add to the pasta in a large serving bowl, top with tomato and nuts and serve.

Golden Delight

SERVES 4

Butternut squash is easy to peel, and by roasting it with onions and sage, you can make a delicious vegetable sauce to go with your favorite pasta, rice, or grain. Use fresh, ripe tomatoes while the season allows, then switch to canned diced tomatoes for a quick, economical, and nutritious winter source. Walnuts add a crunchy note. Cut and sifted sage is not the same as ground sage, which would be too strong in this recipe.

1 lb. butternut squash, peeled and cut into 1-inch pieces, 1/4-inch thick

1 large onion, sliced vertically

1 Tbs. extra-virgin olive oil

1 Tbs. fresh sage, slivered or 1 tsp. cut and sifted dried sage

Salt and freshly ground black pepper, to taste

1/4 cup coarsely chopped walnuts

1/2 lb. dried pasta or 1 cup rice, quinoa, or bulgur

2 cups diced tomato

Freshly grated Parmesan or Romano cheese

Heat the oven to 375°F (191°C). Toss squash and onions with the oil, sage, salt, and pepper on a baking sheet. Spread the vegetables in a single layer and roast for 15 to 20 minutes, stirring once, until the vegetables begin to turn brown. Spread the walnuts on a separate baking sheet and toast in the oven for 5 to 10 minutes, removing when fragrant. Do not let the walnuts burn.

Cook pasta in plenty of boiling water until done but still firm to the bite (al dente). If using grains, cook until tender. Add the roasted vegetables and tomatoes to the pasta or grain. Toss well, sprinkle with walnuts, and serve with Parmesan cheese on the side.

Orzo with Tomato-Artichoke Sauce · SERVES 4 TO 6

Orzo, the rice-shaped pasta, can be replaced with barley or rice in this recipe, or with any other small pasta shape. Make this dish with fresh, ripe tomatoes in season, and feel free to add other vegetables as well. Serve with a green salad or vegetable and a good coarse bread.

½ lb. orzo

1 Tbs. olive oil

3 scallions, chopped

2 cloves garlic, minced

4 cups diced tomatoes

2 14-oz. cans artichoke hearts, drained, rinsed, and coarsely chopped

¼ cup Kalamata olives, pitted and coarsely chopped

1½ tsp. dried oregano or 1½ Tbs. minced fresh oregano

⅛ tsp. ground cinnamon

¼ tsp. freshly ground black pepper

4 oz. feta or ricotta salata cheese, crumbled

Cook pasta in plenty of boiling water until done but still firm to the bite (al dente).

While pasta is cooking, heat the oil in a large nonstick skillet over medium heat. Add the scallions and garlic, and cook, stirring often, for 2 minutes. Add the tomatoes, artichoke hearts, olives, oregano, cinnamon, and pepper. Cook, stirring often, until heated through, about 6 minutes. Top pasta with sauce and cheese, and serve hot.

Macaroni and Cheese with Tomato   SERVES 4

Adding diced tomatoes to macaroni and cheese gives an interesting new taste and color to an old standard. Any sturdy pasta shape will do; don't restrict yourself to elbow macaroni. If you have time, slip the entire dish under the broiler for a few minutes to brown the bread crumbs.

½ lb. twists, penne, gemelli, elbow, or bowtie pasta

2 cups diced tomatoes, drained (save juice)

1 Tbs. olive oil

½ cup chopped scallions

2 cloves garlic, minced

¼ cup flour

2¼ cups skim milk

1 tsp. dried basil or 1 Tbs. minced fresh basil

1 cup shredded low-fat cheddar cheese

¼ cup grated Parmesan cheese

Freshly ground black or white pepper, to taste

Seasoned bread crumbs (optional)

Cook pasta in plenty of boiling water until done but still firm to the bite (al dente). Drain well and return to cooking pot. Stir in tomatoes, cover pot, and keep warm.

While the pasta cooks, heat the oil in a large saucepan over medium heat. Add the scallions and garlic, and sauté for 2 minutes. Add the flour, and mix in with a whisk. Reduce heat and slowly add the milk while mixing constantly with the whisk. Add the basil, and season to taste with pepper. Cook over low heat, stirring constantly, until the sauce thickens and begins to bubble.

Remove from the heat and stir in both cheeses. Add to the macaroni and tomato mixture, and gently combine. Adjust consistency with the reserved tomato juice. If desired, spread in a baking dish or lasagna pan and sprinkle with seasoned bread crumbs; broil about 5 inches from the heat for 1 to 2 minutes to gently toast the bread crumbs before serving.

■ ■ ■

Pasta with Chunky Tomato Sauce SERVES 4

A short cooking time allows tomatoes to keep their fresh flavor in this recipe, while processing them in a blender or food processor allows for a thicker sauce with more body. The carrot adds a natural sweetness.

12 oz. pasta, any shape

4 tsp. olive oil, divided

1 small carrot, diced

1 medium onion, chopped

2 to 4 cloves garlic, minced

1 red bell pepper, chopped

10 large plum tomatoes, peeled and diced

1 tsp. dried basil or 1 Tbs. minced fresh basil

1 tsp. dried oregano or 1 Tbs. minced fresh oregano

Salt and freshly ground black pepper, to taste

Freshly grated Parmesan or Romano cheese

Cook pasta in plenty of boiling water until done but still firm to the bite (al dente).

While the pasta cooks, heat 2 teaspoons of olive oil in a large non-stick skillet over medium heat. Add the diced carrot, and cook for 5 minutes, stirring often to make sure the carrot softens but does not burn. Add the onion, garlic, and red bell pepper, and drizzle the remaining olive oil over all. Toss gently to mix, and cook over medium-high heat, stirring occasionally, for 5 minutes.

Purée about two-thirds of the tomatoes in a blender or food processor until smooth. Add the puréed tomatoes and the remaining diced tomatoes to the vegetables in the skillet, and bring the mixture to a gentle boil. Stir in the herbs, and season to taste with salt and pepper. Reduce the heat and simmer for 5 minutes.

Toss the pasta with a small amount of sauce, and serve with additional sauce and grated cheese.

Portabella Stir-Fry

SERVES 4 TO 6

Portabella mushrooms provide a meaty flavor and texture to meatless meals. In stir-fries, portabellas blend well with any ingredients you would use with meat, including plenty of vegetables, your favorite stir-fry sauce, and "wild" mushrooms such as shiitake, oyster, enoki, and others. Vary the vegetables, and serve over rice, linguine, or any type of Asian noodle.

1 large portabella mushroom cap

1 Tbs. peanut or canola oil

1 medium onion, sliced vertically

1 clove garlic, minced

1 green bell pepper, cut into strips

1 red bell pepper, cut into strips

1 cup sliced green or Savoy cabbage or bok choy

4 oz. shiitake, oyster, or other "wild" mushrooms, stemmed and sliced

4 oz. snow peas or snap peas

1 cup fresh bean sprouts

¼ to ½ cup teriyaki or stir-fry sauce to taste

Cook your choice of rice, linguine, or Asian noodle (see pages 37–40 for instructions).

Wipe the mushroom cap clean and cut in half. Cut across the shorter width into slices roughly ½-inch thick. Prepare all other ingredients and have ready to add to the stir-fry as needed.

Heat the oil in a large nonstick wok or skillet over medium-high heat. Add the onion, and stir-fry for 2 minutes. Add the garlic, portabella mushroom, and green and red bell pepper strips. Stir-fry for 3 minutes. Add the cabbage, and continue to cook for 2 minutes. Add the mushrooms and peas. Stir-fry for 2 minutes more. Add the bean sprouts and sauce. Mix well, and cook until heated through. Serve over rice or noodles.

Sicilian Spirals

SERVES 6

Whole wheat spirals offer good nutrition, a firm texture, and excellent taste. Combine them with the flavors of Sicily: eggplant, peppers, tomatoes, pine nuts, and ricotta salata. Use small eggplants, either baby or Japanese, which are free of bitterness and do not need to be salted and drained.

12 oz. whole wheat spirals

¼ cup pine nuts

1 Tbs. olive oil

1 medium onion, cut in thin half-rings

2 red bell peppers, cut into short strips

2 large baby or Japanese eggplants, cubed

2 large cloves of garlic, chopped

4 cups diced tomatoes

1 Tbs. dried oregano or 2 Tbs. minced fresh oregano

Salt and freshly ground black pepper, to taste

1 oz. ricotta salata, or more to taste, crumbled

Cook the whole wheat spirals in plenty of water until tender but still firm (al dente). Do not overcook. Drain and keep warm.

While pasta is cooking, lightly toast the pine nuts in a dry frying pan. Do not let them burn. Set aside. Heat oil in a large nonstick skillet over medium heat. Add onion and peppers, cover, and cook for 5 minutes. Add cubed eggplant, stir, cover, and cook for 5 minutes more. Add garlic, cover, and cook for 5 minutes. Add tomatoes and oregano, and season to taste with salt and pepper. Mix well, cover, and bring to a boil. Remove cover, lower heat, and simmer for 5 minutes more or until eggplant is cooked. Add toasted pine nuts and mix.

Mix with pasta, crumble ricotta salata over all, and serve.

Vegetable Stroganoff

SERVES 4

Low-fat plain yogurt contributes the creaminess in this recipe; don't use nonfat, as it may separate when cooked. Add your choice of vegetables, and, if you wish, add cooked cubed turkey or ham. Serve over no-yolk "egg" noodles to lower the fat and cholesterol content even more.

12 oz. broad egg noodles	2 tsp. tamari
1 Tbs. olive oil	2 cups low-fat plain yogurt
1 small onion, chopped	¼ cup chopped fresh Italian parsley
½ red bell pepper, chopped	
2 cloves garlic, minced	Skim milk, as needed
4 oz. mushrooms, sliced	Paprika
1 cup cooked corn, peas, carrots, or cut green beans	

Cook the egg noodles according to package directions.

While noodles are cooking, heat the oil in a nonstick skillet over medium heat. Add the onion, pepper, and garlic, and sauté for 5 minutes. Add the mushrooms, and cook for 5 minutes more. Stir in the cooked vegetables and ¼ cup water. (Add more water if mixture appears to be dry.) Cover pan and simmer gently for 10 minutes. (If using cooked meat, add at this point.)

In a small bowl, mix the tamari, yogurt, and parsley. Gently stir into the vegetable mixture. Keep warm but do not allow to boil. Thin with skim milk, if necessary.

Top the drained noodles with the vegetable sauce, and sprinkle lightly with paprika for color.

chicken

Chicken Español

SERVES 4

This recipe uses boneless chicken thighs to speed up the cooking, but you can use chicken legs as long as they are skinless. The original recipe calls for the addition of cooked smoked sausage such as kielbasa or chorizo, sliced and added with the pepper strips. For added Spanish flavor, add 3 or 4 tablespoons of red wine during the last minutes of cooking.

2 Tbs. olive oil

1/2 to 3/4 lb. boneless chicken thighs, cut into bite-sized pieces

1 medium green bell pepper, cut into thin strips

1 small yellow onion, chopped

2 cloves garlic, chopped

1 cup long-grain white rice

1 tsp. turmeric

1/8 tsp. saffron threads (optional)

1 cup crushed tomatoes

1 1/2 cups water

Salt and freshly ground black pepper, to taste

In a large nonstick skillet or Dutch oven, heat the oil over medium-high heat. Add chicken pieces, and stir-fry until lightly browned. Remove the chicken to drain on paper towels. Add peppers to the pan, and sauté for 2 minutes. Remove the peppers, and set aside.

Add the onion, garlic, and rice to the pan, and sauté for 5 minutes. Stir in turmeric and saffron, then add tomatoes and water. Bring to a boil and continue to boil, stirring, for 2 minutes. Add chicken, cover, and reduce the heat to low. Simmer for 15 minutes or until rice is done. Add pepper strips, season to taste, and serve.

Chicken with Pineapple Salsa

SERVES 4

Asian flavors blended with the bite of spicy Mexican salsa produce a tasty combination that is sweet and sharp.

1 cup long-grain white rice or 4 servings instant brown rice, cooked according to package directions

2 tsp. olive oil, divided

3/4 lb. boneless, skinless chicken breast, cut into strips

1 green bell pepper, sliced

4 oz. mushrooms, sliced

1 medium onion, sliced vertically

1 clove garlic, minced

3/4 cup salsa, medium or hot recommended

1 cup pineapple chunks, packed in natural juice

2 tsp. tamari

In a medium saucepan, combine the white rice and 2 cups of water; bring to a boil. Reduce the heat, cover, and simmer for 20 minutes or until all the liquid is absorbed. Keep the pan covered until ready to serve.

While rice is cooking, heat 1 teaspoon of the oil in a large wok or nonstick skillet over high heat. Add the chicken, and stir-fry until firm and opaque, about 5 minutes. Remove the chicken and set it aside.

Add the second teaspoon of oil to the pan. Add the green pepper, mushrooms, and onion, and stir-fry for 5 minutes. Add the garlic, and stir-fry for 1 minute. Return the chicken to the pan. Add the salsa, pineapple, and juice, bring to a boil, lower heat, and cover. Simmer for 2 minutes more. Stir in tamari and serve over rice.

Paprika Chicken with Couscous SERVES 6

This colorful couscous dish can be made vegetarian by eliminating the chicken and using vegetable stock. In either case, steeping the paprika in the stock brings out its color and warm flavor. Modify the recipe with mushrooms, garbanzos, and/or additional vegetables to suit what you have on hand.

2 cups chicken or vegetable stock

1 Tbs. Hungarian sweet paprika

1/4 tsp. freshly ground black pepper

1 cup couscous

1 Tbs. olive oil

1/2 lb. boneless, skinless chicken breast, diced

1 small red onion, chopped

3 scallions, cut into 1/4-inch rounds

1/2 large carrot, cut into large cubes

1/2 red bell pepper, diced

1/2 yellow bell pepper, diced

2 cups diced tomatoes

Salt and freshly ground black pepper, to taste

Bring the stock to a boil in a saucepan with a tight-fitting cover. Remove 1/4 cup of the boiling stock and dissolve the paprika in it. Pour this into the stock remaining in the pot. Add the black pepper and return to a boil. Remove from the heat and add the couscous. Stir, cover, and allow to stand for 5 minutes.

Heat the olive oil in a large nonstick skillet over medium heat. Add the chicken, onion, and scallions. Sauté until the chicken becomes opaque and the onions turn translucent, about 5 minutes. Add the carrot and bell peppers, and sauté for 1 minute. Add the tomato and salt and pepper to taste. Cook for an additional minute, until all ingredients are hot, and remove the pan from the heat.

Add the couscous to the skillet, fluffing it as you mix it in. Serve hot or at room temperature.

Kasha and Chicken Paprikash   SERVES 4

Kasha (toasted buckwheat groats) has a wonderful nutty flavor and a distinctive aroma. Kasha contains all eight essential amino acids as well as B vitamins, vitamin E, iron, potassium, and phosphorous. Egg white is used to keep the grains separate, allowing kasha to be used in pilafs and other dishes as a substitute for rice. This recipe combines kasha with a Hungarian style paprikash that uses low-fat versions of yogurt and sour cream as healthy alternatives to the traditional sour cream. Serve this with a green vegetable such as broccoli or green beans.

1 cup kasha (buckwheat groats)	2 medium onions, chopped
1 egg white	1 green bell pepper, cut in strips
2 cups warm water	1 red bell pepper, cut in strips
2 cups diced tomatoes	2 Tbs. Hungarian sweet paprika
1 Tbs. olive or canola oil	½ cup low-fat sour cream
1 lb. boneless chicken breast, diced or in strips	½ cup low-fat plain yogurt

Mix egg white with kasha in a saucepan, and cook briefly. Add 2 cups water, cover, and bring to a boil. Reduce heat and simmer for 20 minutes, or until water is absorbed.

Drain tomatoes, saving the liquid in a measuring cup. Add water to make 1 cup. While kasha is cooking, heat oil in a large nonstick skillet over medium heat, and add chicken pieces. Sauté for 5 minutes until chicken is opaque. Add onions, bell pepper strips, tomatoes, reserved juice and water, and paprika. Cover and simmer for 20 minutes. Stir in sour cream and yogurt, and warm the mixture but do not boil. Serve with kasha on the side.

Lemon Chicken and Asparagus Stir-Fry

SERVES 4 TO 6

This lemony stir-fry made with slender asparagus spears is a refreshing taste of spring served over white or instant brown rice. Be sure to use an organic lemon for the lemon zest.

1 cup long-grain white rice or 4 servings instant brown rice, cooked according to package directions

1 cup low-sodium chicken stock

2 tsp. cornstarch

1 tsp. tamari

3 Tbs. lemon juice

1 Tbs. grated lemon zest

2 Tbs. canola oil

¾ lb. skinless, boneless chicken breast, cut into thin strips

1 lb. slender asparagus, cut into 1-inch lengths

8 scallions, cut into 1-inch lengths

In a medium saucepan, combine the white rice and 2 cups of water; bring to a boil. Reduce the heat, cover, and simmer for 20 minutes or until all the liquid is absorbed. Keep the pan covered until ready to serve.

While rice is cooking, in a small bowl stir together chicken stock, cornstarch, and tarmari until cornstarch dissolves. Stir in lemon juice and lemon zest. Set aside.

Heat oil in a wok or large nonstick skillet over high heat. Add chicken and asparagus, and stir-fry until chicken is opaque and asparagus is crisp-tender, about 3 minutes. Add scallions, and stir-fry 1 minute. Reduce heat to medium.

Stir sauce mixture again to mix, pour into pan, and cook, stirring, until sauce thickens and turns translucent, about 2 minutes. Serve over rice.

Orange-Asparagus Stir-Fry

SERVES 6

The springtime flavors of asparagus and scallions team up with orange juice, chicken, and pasta to make a hearty meal full of good nutrition. Replace the chicken with shrimp, if you desire, or leave them out entirely for a tasty vegetarian dish. Be sure to use an organic orange for the zest.

12 oz. ziti, mostaccioli, or other medium pasta

2 tsp. canola or olive oil, divided

1/2 lb. boneless, skinless chicken, cut into strips or 12 oz. frozen small shrimp, thawed

3 medium carrots, thinly sliced diagonally

1 lb. asparagus, cut diagonally into 2-inch lengths

1 bunch scallions, chopped

1 cup fresh orange juice

Salt and freshly ground black pepper, to taste

1 Tbs. orange zest, cut into strips (optional)

Cook the pasta in plenty of water until tender but still firm (al dente).

While pasta is cooking, warm 1 teaspoon oil in a large wok or non-stick skillet over high heat. Stir-fry the chicken or shrimp until firm, opaque, and lightly browned, about 3 to 5 minutes. Remove and set aside.

Add the remaining teaspoon of oil to the pan, and stir-fry the carrots for 2 minutes. Add the asparagus and scallions, and stir-fry for another 3 to 4 minutes, until asparagus is tender-crisp.

Add pasta, chicken or shrimp, and orange juice to skillet, and toss about 2 minutes. Season to taste with salt and pepper, and mix in zest, if you choose to use it.

Chicken with Curried Couscous

SERVES 4

Couscous readily takes on flavors, and mixes well with raisins and other dried fruit. In this dish, it's served alongside stir-fried chicken, and would go well with a green vegetable on the side to complete the meal.

CHICKEN:
1 Tbs. olive oil
¾ lb. skinless, boneless chicken breast, cut into strips
2 cloves garlic, minced
¼ cup Worcestershire sauce
2 Tbs. balsamic vinegar
1 cup low-sodium chicken stock
1 tsp. dried oregano or 1 Tbs. minced fresh oregano
Salt and freshly ground black pepper, to taste

COUSCOUS:
1 Tbs. olive oil
1 cup finely chopped onion
2 cloves garlic, minced
¾ tsp. curry powder
1¼ cup low-sodium chicken stock
⅓ cup raisins, golden raisins, or currants
1 Tbs. dried or minced fresh mint
1 cup couscous

Heat 1 tablespoon olive oil in a large nonstick skillet over medium heat. Add the chicken, and sauté until opaque, 3 to 5 minutes. Add garlic, Worcestershire sauce, vinegar, stock, and oregano, and simmer gently, covered, while preparing couscous.

Heat 1 tablespoon olive oil in a saucepan over medium heat. Add onion, and cook for 2 minutes. Reduce heat, add garlic and curry powder, and cook 1 minute. Add stock, raisins, and mint, and bring to a boil. Stir in couscous, cover, remove from heat, and let stand for 5 minutes. Fluff couscous with a fork, and serve with chicken on the side, seasoned to taste with salt and pepper.

Creamy Pesto Chicken

SERVES 6

A blender or food processor makes quick work of turning spinach, basil, and nonfat yogurt into a creamy sauce to be served with lightly sautéed chicken breasts and tubular pasta.

12 oz. ziti, penne, mostaccioli, or elbow macaroni

1 lb. fresh spinach

1/2 cup grated Parmesan cheese

1/2 cup chopped fresh basil

1/4 cup pine nuts

6 cloves garlic, peeled and chopped

1/4 to 1/2 tsp. hot red pepper flakes

1 pint plain nonfat yogurt

Salt, to taste

2 tsp. olive oil

1 medium onion, thinly sliced

1 large red bell pepper, cut into strips

1 lb. skinless, boneless chicken breast, cut into strips

Cook the pasta in plenty of water until tender but still firm (al dente).

While pasta is cooking, combine the spinach, cheese, basil, pine nuts, garlic, red pepper flakes, yogurt, and salt in an electric blender or food processor. Cover and process until smooth.

Heat oil in a large nonstick skillet over medium heat. Add the chicken, onion, and red bell pepper, and cook until chicken is opaque, 3 to 5 minutes. Stir in the spinach mixture, cover, and bring to a simmer. Reduce heat and cook gently until mixture is heated through. Add pasta to the skillet, mix well, and serve.

South-of-the-Border Stir-Fry   SERVES 6

Use this recipe with chicken or fish, or leave them out entirely to make a bean and vegetable stir-fry. Use your favorite fresh, refrigerated, or bottled salsa, and feel free to vary the vegetables as available.

1 cup long-grain white rice or 4 servings instant brown rice, cooked according to package directions

2 Tbs. lime juice

1/4 cup water

1 1/2 tsp. cornstarch

1/2 tsp. chili powder

1 Tbs. olive oil

1/2 lb. boneless, skinless chicken breast, cut into strips or 1/2 lb. firm white fish cut into cubes

2 cups chopped vegetables, such as broccoli, corn, or bell peppers

2 cups cooked black beans, rinsed and drained if canned

1/3 cup salsa

2 Tbs. minced cilantro

In a medium saucepan, combine the white rice and 2 cups of water; bring to a boil. Reduce the heat, cover, and simmer for 20 minutes or until all the liquid is absorbed. Keep the pan covered until ready to serve.

Combine lime juice, water, cornstarch, and chili powder, and set aside. Heat oil in a wok or nonstick skillet over high heat, and add chicken or fish. Stir-fry until surface is opaque and chicken or fish is cooked through, 3 to 5 minutes. Add vegetables, and stir-fry for 2 minutes. Add beans and salsa, mix well, and heat through. Add lime juice mixture, and cook, stirring until thickened. Stir in cilantro, and serve over rice.

Chicken Palermo SERVES 6

The flavors of Sicily—anchovies, capers, raisins, and pine nuts—combine with tomatoes, onions, and garlic to produce a rich-tasting sauce for your choice of pasta, couscous, or rice. For the anchovy-conscious, rest assured that the anchovies dissolve in the sauce, leaving no identifiable trace, but contribute to the distinctive flavor and should not be left out.

12 oz. pasta, 1½ cups rice, or 1½ cups couscous

2 Tbs. pine nuts

2 Tbs. olive oil, divided

¾ lb. skinless, boneless chicken breast, cut into ¾-inch cubes

1 medium onion, diced

4 cloves garlic, minced

6 anchovy filets

4 cups diced tomato

2 Tbs. balsamic vinegar

1 Tbs. capers, rinsed

3 Tbs. golden raisins

Freshly ground black pepper, to taste

Cook pasta, rice, or couscous, timing it to be ready when the sauce is complete.

While the pasta or rice cooks, lightly toast the pine nuts in a dry skillet until golden. Set aside to cool.

Heat 1 tablespoon of oil in a large nonstick skillet over medium heat. Add the chicken pieces, and cook until chicken is opaque, 3 to 5 minutes. Add remaining oil, onion, and garlic, and sauté for 3 minutes. Add anchovies, and cook, stirring until anchovies break up. Add remaining ingredients, and bring to a gentle simmer. Cook, uncovered, for 15 minutes, stirring occasionally. Stir in pine nuts and serve over cooked pasta or rice.

Apple Harvest Chicken

SERVES 4

My mother made this recipe with pork chops when I was growing up. I have substituted chicken for a quick version that goes nicely over fettucine.

½ lb. dry or 12 oz. fresh spinach fettucine

2 tsp. canola oil

¾ lb. boneless, skinless chicken breast, cut into ¾-inch cubes

4 oz. mushrooms, sliced

1 large onion, thinly sliced

2 medium baking apples, peeled and thinly sliced

½ cup apple juice or cider

1 tsp. dried basil or 1 Tbs. minced fresh basil

8 oz. low-fat or nonfat sour cream

Salt and freshly ground black pepper, to taste

Paprika

Cook pasta in plenty of boiling water until done but still firm to the bite (al dente).

While pasta is cooking, heat oil in a large nonstick skillet over medium heat. Add chicken cubes, and sauté until opaque on all sides, 3 to 5 minutes. Add mushrooms, and sauté for 2 to 3 minutes more. Add onion, apples, apple juice, and basil. Cover, bring to a boil, reduce heat, and simmer until apples are tender (about 10 minutes). Gently stir in sour cream, and warm through. Season to taste with salt and pepper.

Place fettucine on a platter and spoon chicken mixture over the top. Sprinkle with paprika and serve.

Quick Jambalaya

SERVES 4

North Country Smokehouse in Claremont, New Hampshire, uses their spicy andouille sausage in this Louisiana specialty. Serve jambalaya in honor of Mardi Gras or whenever the urge for Cajun or Creole food strikes your fancy. You can also add shrimp during the last 10 minutes of cooking.

½ lb. skinless, boneless chicken breast, diced

2 cups water

½ lb. andouille sausage, sliced and halved

7 cups crushed tomatoes

1 large onion, chopped

2 green bell peppers, seeded and chopped

2 tsp. freshly ground black pepper

1 tsp. chili powder

1 tsp. garlic powder

½ tsp. cayenne pepper

¼ tsp. hot pepper sauce

1 cup long-grain white rice

In a large saucepan, poach the diced chicken in the water until opaque, about 5 minutes. Add the remaining ingredients, except for the rice, and bring to a boil, stirring occasionally. Reduce the heat and add the rice. Cover and simmer for 20 minutes. Serve immediately.

Hungarian Chicken

SERVES 4

When available, use the long, pale green cubanelle peppers for the most authentic flavor, and don't forget the paprika and caraway for the Hungarian accent. The cornstarch keeps the yogurt from separating.

8 oz. egg noodles, medium or broad

1 Tbs. olive oil

1 large onion, chopped

3/4 lb. skinless, boneless chicken breast, cut into 1/2-inch-wide strips

4 cubanelle or other long Italian-type peppers, diced

2 cloves garlic, minced

4 cups crushed tomatoes

2 tsp. caraway seeds

2 tsp. Hungarian sweet paprika

1 cup fat-free plain yogurt

1 Tbs. cornstarch

Cook noodles according to package directions; drain and reserve 1 cup of cooking water.

While the noodles are cooking, heat the oil in a large nonstick skillet over medium heat. Add the onion, and cook for 3 minutes. Add the chicken, and cook until opaque, 3 to 5 minutes. Add the peppers, garlic, tomatoes, caraway seeds, and paprika. Cover and cook for 10 minutes or until the chicken is cooked through and the peppers are soft.

Mix a little of the yogurt with the cornstarch until smooth, then stir into the remaining yogurt. Stir into the chicken mixture and cook just until the sauce thickens. Use the reserved noodle water to adjust sauce consistency, if necessary. Serve chicken over cooked noodles.

■ ■ ■

Chicken and Vegetable Couscous

SERVES 6

Couscous comes in both whole wheat and refined wheat forms; the cooking time is the same for both. Use couscous wherever you would use rice, for a change of pace and nutrition.

1 Tbs. olive oil

3/4 lb. boneless, skinless chicken breast, cut into 3/4-inch cubes

1/2 cup chopped green onions

3 cloves garlic, minced

4 cups diced tomatoes

2 cups cooked garbanzo beans, rinsed and drained if canned

8 oz. baby carrots, cut into coins

1 small yellow squash, chopped

1/2 red bell pepper, chopped

1/4 cup golden or regular raisins

2 tsp. ground cumin

3/4 tsp. ground cinnamon

1 1/2 cups chicken stock or water

1 cup uncooked couscous

Heat oil in a large nonstick skillet over medium heat. Add chicken, and sauté until opaque, about 5 minutes. Add onions and garlic, and cook for 1 minute. Stir in remaining ingredients, except stock and couscous. Bring to a simmer and cook for 15 minutes.

Bring the stock or water to a boil and stir in the couscous. Cover, remove from the heat, and let sit for 5 minutes. Fluff the couscous with a fork. Serve the chicken and vegetables over individual servings of the couscous.

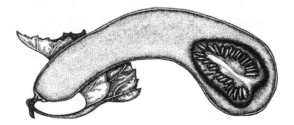

Maple Season Stir-Fry

SERVES 4

Maple syrup glazes the chicken with a deep, dark sauce that complements your choice of stir-fry vegetables.

1 cup long-grain white rice or 4 servings instant brown rice, cooked according to package directions

1 Tbs. canola oil

3/4 lb. boneless, skinless chicken breast, cut into strips

1 medium onion, sliced vertically

1 red bell pepper, sliced into thin strips

4 cloves garlic, minced

4 oz. mushrooms, sliced

1/2 cup maple syrup

1/4 cup tamari

1/4 cup sherry, apple juice, or water

2 Tbs. cornstarch

1/2 tsp. ground ginger or 1 tsp. grated fresh gingerroot

Dash of cayenne pepper

1/4 cup unsalted, roasted cashews (optional)

In a medium saucepan, combine the white rice and 2 cups of water; bring to a boil. Reduce the heat, cover, and simmer for 20 minutes or until all the liquid is absorbed. Keep the pan covered until ready to serve.

While rice is cooking, heat the oil in a large wok or nonstick skillet over high heat. Add the chicken strips, and sauté until chicken is opaque, about 5 minutes. Add onion, pepper, garlic, and mushrooms, and stir-fry until crisp-tender, about 5 minutes.

Combine maple syrup, tamari, sherry, cornstarch, ginger, and cayenne in a small bowl. Add to chicken and vegetables. Continue cooking and stirring until mixture thickens and develops a glaze, about 3 minutes. Stir in cashews and serve over rice.

Chicken and Roasted Peppers   SERVES 6

This delicious and easy dish takes advantage of the sweetness of slow-cooked onions, roasted red peppers, and balsamic vinegar to highlight the chicken and pasta.

¾ lb. boneless, skinless chicken breast, cut into ¾-inch cubes

¼ cup balsamic vinegar

12 oz. medium pasta, such as rotini, penne, or gemelli

2 Tbs. olive oil

1 medium onion, cut vertically into thin slices

4 red bell peppers, roasted, peeled, and cut into short strips

½ tsp. hot red pepper flakes, or to taste

2 cups diced tomatoes

Salt and freshly ground black pepper, to taste

Freshly grated Parmesan or Romano cheese

Mix the chicken pieces with the balsamic vinegar, stirring to coat them well.

Cook pasta in plenty of boiling water until done but still firm to the bite (al dente).

While the pasta cooks, heat the oil in a large nonstick skillet over medium heat. Add the onion, and sauté for 5 minutes. Add the marinated chicken, and cook until opaque, about 5 minutes. Add the roasted peppers and hot red pepper flakes, cover, and cook for 5 minutes. Stir in the tomatoes, and mix well. Cover and cook for 5 minutes. Season to taste with salt and pepper, toss with drained pasta, and serve with grated cheese.

Luau Chicken

SERVES 4

This quick and easy stir-fry, with a touch of sweet, tart, and spicy, works equally well with fish such as halibut, tilapia, sea bass, or haddock. Add your favorite vegetables in season, including broccoli florets, green or yellow beans, or sliced cucumber for added crunch.

1 cup long-grain white rice or 4 servings instant brown rice, cooked according to package directions

1 Tbs. canola or peanut oil

1 clove garlic, minced

2 tsp. curry powder

¾ lb. skinless, boneless chicken breast, cut into strips

1 large green bell pepper, diced

1 bunch scallions, sliced

¼ lb. edible pea pods or snap peas

1 20-oz. can unsweetened pineapple chunks, with juice

2 Tbs. lemon juice

1 Tbs. cornstarch in 2 Tbs. water

In a medium saucepan, combine the white rice and 2 cups of water; bring to a boil. Reduce the heat, cover, and simmer for 20 minutes or until all the liquid is absorbed. Keep the pan covered until ready to serve.

While rice is cooking, heat the oil in a large nonstick skillet or wok over medium heat. Add the garlic, and sauté for 1 minute. Stir in the curry powder, and cook until frothy. Add the chicken strips, and cook for 3 minutes. Add the green pepper, scallions, and peas, and stir-fry for 1 minute. Stir in pineapple, lemon juice, and half of the cornstarch mixture. Cook, adding more cornstarch mixture as needed to produce a thick sauce. Fluff the rice with a fork and serve chicken mixture over rice.

Chicken Sausage Sauté
SERVES 6

*This quick and easy dish uses all those aromatic ingredients that draw peo-
ple into the kitchen to see what's for supper. It's an easy sauté of garlic,
onions, bell peppers, and tasty chicken sausage, served with your favorite
pasta. Use the chicken sausage of your choice, including sausages flavored
with herbs, sun-dried tomatoes, apples, or spices.*

12 oz. linguine, spaghetti,
fettucine, spirals, or penne

4 chicken sausages

2 Tbs. olive oil

1 medium onion, cut vertically
into thin slices

2 red or yellow bell peppers, cut
into ½-inch strips

4 cloves garlic, chopped

1 tsp. crushed dried rosemary or
1 Tbs. minced fresh rosemary

Freshly ground black pepper, to
taste

2 Tbs. balsamic vinegar

Cook pasta in plenty of boiling water until done but still firm to the bite
(al dente).

While the pasta is cooking, place the sausages in a small skillet over
medium heat and add ¼ cup water. Cover and simmer for 10 minutes.
Turn sausages at 5 minutes, and add more water if necessary.

While the sausages cook, heat the oil in a large nonstick skillet over
medium heat. Add the onion and bell pepper strips, and sauté for 10
minutes. Add the garlic and rosemary, and season with black pepper to
taste. Lower heat and cook for 5 minutes more. Remove sausages from
small skillet and slice in half lengthwise, then crosswise into ½-inch
slices. Add to the onion and pepper. Add balsamic vinegar, and toss.
Cook mixture until sausage is no longer pink in the middle. Serve over
cooked pasta.

Chicken Fajita

SERVES 4

A true Texas fajita is strips of marinated skirt steak served on tortillas. Our version is lightly marinated chicken strips cooked with peppers, onions, and garlic. Fresh cilantro, cumin, and lime juice add the Tex-Mex touch. For a spicy variation, add one minced chipotle pepper to the chicken mixture before it is cooked.

¼ cup fresh lime juice

3 cloves garlic, minced

¼ cup chopped cilantro, divided

1 tsp. dried oregano or 1 Tbs. minced fresh oregano

1 tsp. dried basil or 1 Tbs. minced fresh basil

1 tsp. ground cumin

Freshly ground black pepper, to taste

1 tsp. cornstarch

¾ lb. boneless, skinless chicken breast, cut into thin strips

1 Tbs. olive oil

1 red bell pepper, cut into thin strips

1 green bell pepper, cut into thin strips

1 medium red onion, cut vertically into thin slices

⅓ cup low sodium chicken stock

Corn or flour tortillas, warmed

In a medium bowl, whisk together the lime juice, garlic, 2 tablespoons of the cilantro, oregano, basil, cumin, black pepper, and cornstarch. Add the chicken, and toss to coat. Let sit for 5 minutes.

Heat the oil in a large nonstick skillet over medium-high heat. Add the bell peppers and onion, and sauté for 2 minutes. Add the chicken and its marinade, and cook, stirring frequently, for 5 minutes. Add the stock, and cook, stirring constantly, for 2 minutes. Remove from the heat and stir in the remaining 2 tablespoons of cilantro. Spoon the chicken mixture on top of warm tortillas, roll it up like a burrito, and serve.

Potatoes, Peppers, and Chicken Sausage

SERVES 4

Sausage can be part of a healthy meal when it is a flavor component rather than the main ingredient. Chicken or turkey sausage is a leaner choice than pork, and the new sausages on the market come in an appealing array of flavors. Many of these sausages are not precooked; be sure to cook them thoroughly by steaming first, then browning as described.

2 chicken sausages, any flavor

1 lb. small red potatoes, scrubbed and thinly sliced

1 Tbs. plus 2 tsp. olive oil, divided

1 large Spanish or Vidalia onion, chopped

2 cloves garlic, minced

1 red bell pepper, cut into thin strips

1 green bell pepper, cut into thin strips

4 cups diced tomato

Salt and freshly ground black pepper, to taste

Place the sausages in a small skillet. Add ¼ cup water, cover, and simmer over medium heat for 10 minutes. Turn sausages at 5 minutes and add more water if necessary.

Heat 1 tablespoon oil in a large nonstick skillet over medium heat, and add the potato slices. Sauté, flipping the potatoes occasionally until they begin to brown, about 5 minutes. Add the onion, garlic, and pepper strips, mix well, and cover. Reduce heat and cook gently for 10 minutes. Add the tomatoes and their juices, cover, and cook for 10 minutes more or until vegetables are soft.

Meanwhile, remove the cover from the sausage pan and add 2 teaspoons of oil. Cook over medium-high heat until the water evaporates and the sausages begin to brown. Turn to brown evenly, then slice one open lengthwise to ensure that it is cooked. Remove cooked sausages from pan, slice lengthwise, then crosswise into ¼-inch slices. Add to vegetables, mix gently, add salt and pepper to taste, and serve.

Creamy Ricotta Chicken   SERVES 6

Sweetly bland ricotta cheese, added at the last minute to this combination of penne, chicken, and vegetables, produces a creamy sauce that adds subtle flavor, as well as calcium, to the dish. Without the chicken, this is equally good as a vegetarian main dish or as a pasta component of a larger meal. If mint is not available, fresh basil can be substituted. Do not use dried herbs for this recipe.

12 oz. penne, ziti, or twists

4 cups diced tomato

¼ cup chopped fresh Italian parsley

¼ cup chopped fresh mint

3 cloves garlic, minced

¼ cup extra-virgin olive oil

1 Tbs. olive oil

¾ lb. boneless, skinless chicken breast, cut into ¾-inch cubes

½ cup ricotta cheese

2 oz. ricotta salata cheese, crumbled (optional)

Freshly grated Romano or Parmesan cheese

Cook pasta in plenty of boiling water until done but still firm to the bite (al dente).

While the pasta cooks, combine the tomatoes, parsley, mint, and garlic in a bowl. Add the ¼ cup of extra-virgin olive oil. Mix well and set aside.

Heat the tablespoon of oil in a large nonstick skillet over medium heat. Add the chicken, and sauté until opaque, about 5 minutes. Lower the heat, cover, and cook for 5 minutes more or until the centers of the cubes are no longer pink.

Add the tomato mixture to the chicken and bring to a gentle simmer. Add the drained pasta, and mix well. Spoon the ricotta cheese over the top and cover the pan. Cook over low heat for 1 minute to warm the cheese. Gently mix the ricotta into the pasta mixture to coat the other ingredients. Mix in the ricotta salata, and serve hot with grated cheese on the side.

Lemon Chicken Couscous   SERVES 4

If you have the time to plan ahead, be sure to try this as a cold salad. It can also be served as a vegetarian dish, or a seafood salad by replacing the chicken with small cooked shrimp.

2½ cups low-sodium chicken stock

4 oz. boneless, skinless chicken breast, cut into ¾-inch cubes

1½ cups couscous

¼ cup fresh lemon juice

¼ cup extra-virgin olive oil

Freshly ground black pepper, to taste

½ lb. fresh spinach, stems discarded, leaves finely chopped

3 scallions, sliced thin

3 tablespoons finely chopped fresh dill weed

Bring the stock to a boil in a large saucepan, and add the chicken pieces. Reduce to a simmer and cook for 5 minutes or until the chicken is cooked through and no pink centers remain. Remove the chicken with a slotted spoon and refrigerate.

Return the stock to a boil. Remove from the heat and stir in the couscous. Cover and let stand for 5 minutes or until all liquid is absorbed. Fluff the couscous with a fork and transfer to a bowl.

In a small bowl, whisk together the lemon juice, oil, and black pepper. Add to couscous, and mix. Stir in the chicken, spinach, scallions, and dill. Serve immediately or refrigerate.

Turkey

Orzo Olé

SERVES 4

Fresh salsa provides the garlic and fresh tomato taste that blends so well with Mexican seasonings. Ground turkey is a low-fat alternative to beef that can easily be left out for a no-meat meal.

1/2 lb. orzo

1 tsp. canola or olive oil

3/4 lb. ground turkey

1 medium onion, coarsely chopped

1 green bell pepper, chopped

2 cups diced tomatoes

2 cups fresh salsa

1/2 tsp. dried oregano or 1 1/2 tsp. minced fresh oregano

4 cups cooked black beans, drained and rinsed if canned

1 1/2 tsp. chili powder, or more to taste

5 drops hot red pepper sauce

1 Tbs. coarsely chopped cilantro

Cook the orzo in plenty of boiling water until done but still firm to the bite (al dente).

While the orzo is cooking, heat the oil in a large nonstick skillet over medium heat. Add the ground turkey, and cook, stirring, for 5 minutes. Add the onion and green pepper, and sauté until onion is translucent, about 5 minutes more. Add the tomatoes, salsa, and oregano. Bring to a boil, lower the heat, cover, and simmer for 5 minutes. Add the beans, and cook until beans are heated through. Season to taste with chili powder, red pepper sauce, and cilantro, and mix well. Stir into drained orzo and serve.

Texas Hash

SERVES 4

Vegetables, rice, and lean ground turkey combine in a single pan that then goes under the broiler for a melted cheese finish. Vary the recipe by substituting your favorite salsa for the tomatoes, use instant brown rice, or add fresh cut green beans in season.

½ cup Texmati or other long-grain white rice

2 cups low-sodium chicken stock, divided

2 tsp. olive oil

8 oz. ground turkey

1 large onion, diced

1 large green bell pepper, diced

2 cups crushed tomatoes, with juice

1 cup cooked corn

1 Tbs. chili powder

1 cup shredded Monterey Jack cheese or reduced fat cheddar cheese

In a medium saucepan, combine the white rice and 1 cup of stock; bring to a boil. Reduce the heat, cover, and simmer for 20 minutes or until all the liquid is absorbed. Keep the pan covered until ready to serve.

While the rice cooks, heat the oil in a large nonstick skillet over medium heat. Add the ground turkey, and cook, stirring to crumble, for 5 minutes. Add the remaining cup of stock, and stir to dissolve any brown from the bottom of the pan. Add the onion and green pepper, bring to a simmer, and cook for 5 minutes. Add the tomatoes, corn, and chili powder; mix well, bring to a simmer, cover, and cook for 10 minutes.

Preheat the broiler. Add the cooked rice to the turkey mixture and mix well. Top with the shredded cheese, and put under the broiler just long enough to melt the cheese. Serve hot.

Chili Skillet Dinner

SERVES 4

Mild chilis and cilantro are the main flavors in this quick skillet dinner that can be served over fresh or dried pasta, egg noodles, or your favorite grain. Here they are combined with smoked turkey or chicken and artichoke hearts to make a colorful dish that is also hearty and full of flavor. When working with the chili peppers, be sure to wear gloves. Remove the seeds and inner ribs to modify the heat from the peppers.

8 oz. broad egg noodles

1 Tbs. olive oil

4 oz. mushrooms, sliced

3 Tbs. minced mild green chilis (Poblano or Anaheim), or to taste

1/2 red bell pepper, diced

1 can artichoke hearts, rinsed, drained, squeezed dry, and quartered

4 oz. smoked turkey or chicken, cut into cubes

3 Tbs. chopped cilantro

1/3 cup nonfat or low-fat sour cream

Salt and freshly ground black pepper, to taste

Cook the noodles according to package directions. Drain, saving 1 cup of the water in which the noodles were cooked.

While the noodles cook, heat the oil in a large nonstick skillet over medium heat. Add the mushrooms, chilis, and red pepper. Cook, stirring frequently, for 5 minutes. Add the artichoke hearts, and cook 5 minutes longer. Add the turkey or chicken and the cilantro. Cook for 2 minutes, or until heated through. Remove from the heat and stir in the sour cream. Season to taste with salt and pepper. Add the drained noodles to the skillet and toss well. Add noodle water, as needed, to make a creamy sauce, and serve.

Bacon, Pancetta, or Sausage

Pasta Trattoria Style   SERVES 6

The finished dish should be full of color and texture, so don't chop the vegetables too small. Use a medium-sized pasta shape with hollows to catch the bits of sauce, and cook the sauce quickly, as part of its appeal is its fresh taste. The bacon provides a nice smoky flavor, but can be eliminated if you prefer.

12 oz. medium-sized shells, farfalle, gnocchi, or rotelle

1/4 lb. slab bacon, cut into thick slices and coarsely chopped

2 Tbs. olive oil

2 small onions, coarsely chopped

3/4 lb. mushrooms, thinly sliced

4 cups diced tomatoes

1 14-oz. can artichoke hearts, rinsed and drained

Freshly ground black pepper, to taste

1/3 cup coarsely chopped Italian parsley

1 tsp. dried thyme or 1 Tbs. fresh thyme

2 tsp. dried oregano or 2 Tbs. minced fresh oregano

3 oz. ricotta salata cheese, grated or crumbled

Cook pasta in plenty of boiling water until done but still firm to the bite (al dente).

While pasta is cooking, squeeze excess water from artichoke hearts and cut into quarters.

Sauté chopped bacon in a large saucepan until brown. Remove to drain on paper towels, discard fat from pan, and wipe pan clean. Add olive oil, and heat over medium heat. Add onions and mushrooms, and sauté for 5 minutes. Add tomatoes and artichoke hearts, and season with black pepper to taste. If using dried herbs, add at this point. Bring mixture to a boil, reduce heat, and simmer for 15 minutes. If using fresh herbs, add and cook for 5 minutes more. Add drained pasta and ricotta salata, mix well, and serve.

Brazilian Beans and Rice

SERVES 4

Feijoada (fay-ZHWAH-dah) is Brazil's most famous national dish. In this version, we use precooked black beans to speed up the preparation time. Serve with white rice or instant brown rice for a quick and hearty meal with South American flair.

1 cup long-grain white rice or 4 servings instant brown rice, cooked according to package directions

2 tsp. olive oil

1 medium onion, chopped

1/4 lb. kielbasa, linguica, or chorizo, cut into 1/2-inch cubes

1/2 tsp. cumin

1 large garlic clove, minced

2 cups cooked black beans, drained and rinsed if canned

1 1/2 cups water

Freshly ground black pepper, to taste

1 bay leaf

1 Tbs. red or white wine vinegar

1/2 tsp. hot pepper sauce, or more to taste

In a medium saucepan, combine the white rice and 2 cups of water; bring to a boil. Reduce the heat, cover, and simmer for 20 minutes or until all the liquid is absorbed. Keep the pan covered until ready to serve.

While rice is cooking, heat oil in a large saucepan or Dutch oven over medium heat. Add onion and sausage, and sauté for 5 minutes. Add cumin and garlic, and sauté for 1 minute. Add beans, water, black pepper, and bay leaf. Mix and bring to a boil. Cover, reduce heat, and simmer for 15 minutes.

Remove bay leaf, and stir in vinegar and hot pepper sauce. Serve over cooked rice.

Pasta with Garden Tomato and Onion Sauce

SERVES 6

This simple late-harvest sauce is made of fresh tomatoes and red onions cooked until they are thick and fragrant. Pancetta is a lean Italian bacon that is not smoked but gets its flavor from a spice and salt cure. If pancetta is not available, use Canadian bacon, or eliminate meat altogether.

12 oz. spaghetti or linguine

2 tsp. plus 1 Tbs. olive oil, divided

¼ lb. pancetta, sliced thick, finely chopped

¼ tsp. hot red pepper flakes

1 large red onion, coarsely chopped

3 large ripe tomatoes, peeled, seeded, chopped, and drained of excess liquid

Freshly grated Romano or Parmesan cheese

Cook pasta in plenty of boiling water until done but still firm to the bite (al dente).

While the pasta cooks, heat 2 teaspoons of the olive oil in a heavy saucepan over medium heat. Add the pancetta, and cook for 5 minutes, stirring constantly, until the pieces are crisp. Pour off any excess fat. Add the tablespoon of oil, then the pepper flakes and onion. Sauté for 5 minutes. Add the tomatoes, and sauté for 1 minute. Lower the heat, cover, and simmer for 10 minutes. Uncover and cook for 5 minutes more or until excess liquid evaporates and sauce is thick. Add drained pasta to the sauce and mix well. Serve with grated cheese on the side.

Beef

Southwestern Skillet
SERVES 4

Pinto beans, wagon wheel pasta, and the flavors of the American Southwest make this a fun dish for kids as well as adults. The ground beef is optional, or could be replaced by ground turkey, and you can modify the "heat" by using more or less hot pepper sauce.

1/2 lb. wagon wheel pasta

4 tsp. olive oil, divided

4 oz. ground round

1 small onion, finely chopped

1 green bell pepper, finely chopped

1 garlic clove, minced

2 cups cooked pinto beans, drained and rinsed if canned

4 cups diced tomatoes

Hot red pepper sauce, to taste

1 Tbs. coarsely chopped cilantro

Salt and freshly ground black pepper, to taste

1/4 cup grated low-fat cheddar cheese

Cook pasta in plenty of boiling water until done but still firm to the bite (al dente).

While pasta cooks, heat 2 teaspoons of oil in a large nonstick skillet over low heat. Add ground round, and cook, stirring, until brown and crumbly. Remove to a colander and rinse under hot water to remove excess fat. Wipe out pan, add remaining 2 teaspoons of oil, and place over medium heat. Add onion, green pepper, and garlic. Sauté for 3 minutes. Add cooked beef, beans, and tomatoes, and bring to a simmer. Stir in hot pepper sauce and cilantro, and adjust seasonings with salt and pepper. Add drained wagon wheels, mix well, and transfer to a serving dish. Sprinkle with cheddar cheese and serve.

Spicy Sesame Beef Stir-Fry

SERVES 4

Use your favorite mix of stir-fry vegetables including cabbage, broccoli, carrots, and peppers along with edible pea pods or snap peas for interest and added nutrition.

1/2 lb. Asian noodles or linguine

1/4 cup tamari

2 Tbs. minced fresh gingerroot

2 cloves garlic, minced

1/4 tsp. hot red pepper flakes

2 tsp. cornstarch

3/4 cup water

3/4 lb. lean boneless beef, such as sirloin or top round

3 Tbs. sesame seeds

2 Tbs. peanut or canola oil, divided

1 small onion, sliced vertically

3 to 4 cups bite-sized pieces of broccoli, carrots, cabbage, and bell peppers

Handful of edible pea pods or snap peas

Prepare noodles or linguine according to package directions.

While noodles are cooking, whisk together the tamari, gingerroot, garlic, hot red pepper flakes, cornstarch, and water in a small bowl. Cut the beef across the grain into very thin strips and sprinkle with sesame seeds, tossing to coat evenly. Heat 1 tablespoon of the oil in a wok or large nonstick skillet over high heat. Add beef, and stir-fry until brown, about 2 minutes. Remove with a slotted spoon to a plate. Heat remaining tablespoon of oil in same skillet. Add onion, vegetable mix, and peas, and stir-fry until vegetables are crisp-tender, about 4 minutes. Reduce heat to medium. Stir tamari mixture to blend, then add to pan along with cooked beef and any accumulated juices. Cook, stirring, until sauce thickens and becomes translucent, about 2 minutes. Serve at once over hot noodles or linguine.

Pasta Calabrese

SERVES 6

Lean beef seasoned with fennel and red pepper flakes mimics the flavor of spicy Italian sausage while eliminating the fat that sausage contributes. For variety, add green bell peppers or canned artichoke hearts that have been quartered.

12 oz. medium pasta (gemelli, penne, rotini)

2 tsp. olive oil

¾ lb. ground round

1 medium onion, diced

1 clove garlic, minced

1 tsp. fennel seeds, crushed

¼ tsp. hot red pepper flakes

4 cups crushed tomatoes

Salt and freshly ground black pepper, to taste

Freshly grated Parmesan or Romano cheese

Cook pasta in plenty of boiling water until done but still firm to the bite (al dente).

While pasta is cooking, heat oil in a large nonstick skillet over medium heat. Add the ground round, onion, garlic, fennel seeds, and red pepper flakes, and cook until the meat is well browned and crumbly and the onions are soft, about 5 minutes. Stir in tomatoes, and bring to a boil. Reduce heat, cover, and simmer 10 minutes. Taste for salt and pepper, and adjust. Serve over cooked pasta with grated cheese on the side.

Beef Stir-Fry Italienne

SERVES 4

Lean beef can be part of a healthful meal, especially when it is grilled, broiled, or stir-fried with a minimum of added fat. A small amount of beef adds flavor to this dish made primarily with vegetables and pasta, conserving both fat calories and dollars.

8 oz. spaghetti, linguine, or vermicelli

4 tsp. olive oil, divided

1/2 lb. lean boneless sirloin or top round, trimmed of all visible fat, cut in half lengthwise and thinly sliced

1 medium onion, thinly sliced

3 cloves garlic, minced

1 red or green bell pepper, thinly sliced

8 oz. mushrooms, sliced

1/2 pint cherry tomatoes, halved

1 Tbs. red wine vinegar

1 Tbs. balsamic vinegar

1/4 tsp. dried or 3/4 tsp. minced fresh thyme

1/4 tsp. dried or 3/4 tsp. minced fresh oregano

1/4 tsp. dried or 3/4 tsp. minced fresh basil

Freshly grated Parmesan or Romano cheese

Cook pasta in plenty of boiling water until done but still firm to the bite (al dente). Drain and reserve 1/2 cup pasta water.

While pasta is cooking, heat 2 teaspoons of oil in a large nonstick skillet over medium heat. Add the beef slices, and stir-fry until brown, about 2 minutes. Remove with a slotted spoon to a plate. Pour off excess fat and wipe pan dry. Add the remaining 2 teaspoons of oil to the skillet, and stir-fry the onion, garlic, pepper, and mushrooms for 5 minutes. Return the beef and any accumulated juices to skillet, along with the tomato halves, vinegars, and herbs. Heat through, but do not overcook. Adjust to a saucelike consistency with reserved pasta water, as needed. Serve over hot pasta with grated cheese on the side.

Beef Shiitake Stir-Fry

SERVES 4

This recipe takes advantage of lean sirloin or top round steak and fresh shiitake mushrooms to make a sukiyaki-style stir-fry to be served over rice, linguine, or Japanese (udon or soba) noodles.

1 cup long-grain white rice or 4 servings instant brown rice, cooked according to package directions or 8 oz. Japanese noodles or linguine

1½ cups low-sodium beef stock

2 Tbs. tamari

¼ cup sherry or apple juice

1 tsp. sugar

2 Tbs. canola or peanut oil, divided

1 lb. lean boneless sirloin or top round, trimmed of all visible fat, cut in half lengthwise and thinly sliced

1 onion, cut in half lengthwise, then thinly sliced

4 oz. shiitake mushrooms, stems discarded, caps cut into ¼-inch strips

½ lb. spinach, stems discarded, cut into thin strips

2 cups fresh mung bean sprouts

2 Tbs. cornstarch dissolved in 3 Tbs. water

In a medium saucepan, combine the white rice and 2 cups of water; bring to a boil. Reduce the heat, cover, and simmer for 20 minutes or until all the liquid is absorbed. Keep the pan covered until ready to serve. If using noodles, cook according to package directions.

Whisk together the stock, tamari, sherry or juice, and sugar in a small bowl.

Heat 2 teaspoons of oil in a large nonstick skillet over high heat. Add half the beef and cook, stirring, until browned on all sides, about 2 minutes. Remove with a slotted spoon to a plate. Add another 2 teaspoons of oil, if needed, and repeat with remaining beef. Set browned beef aside.

Add remaining oil to skillet and heat. Add onion and mushrooms, and stir-fry for 3 minutes. Stir the tamari mixture once more and add it to the pan. Stir in the cornstarch mixture, a little at a time, until the sauce is slightly thickened. All the cornstarch may not be needed. Layer the spinach and sprouts over the beef, cover, and cook 1 minute. Toss gently and serve over hot rice or noodles.

■ ■ ■

Satay-Style Beef

SERVES 4

Satay is an Indonesian specialty, consisting of marinated meat, fish, or poultry cubes threaded on skewers and grilled or broiled, then served with a spicy peanut sauce. This recipe uses bottled teriyaki sauce combined with peanut butter for a quick satay-style sauce that gives a satisfying combination of flavors in a short amount of time. Be sure to serve this dish with a mixed salad of greens and fresh vegetables on the side for good nutrition.

½ lb. lean boneless sirloin or top round, trimmed of all visible fat, cut in half lengthwise and thinly sliced

2 Tbs. plus ¼ cup bottled teriyaki sauce, divided

12 oz. Chinese cellophane or rice noodles, linguine, or spaghetti

3 Tbs. creamy peanut butter

2 Tbs. water

¼ tsp. ground ginger or 1 tsp. grated gingerroot

Pinch of hot red pepper flakes

2 tsp. canola or peanut oil

1 medium cucumber, seeded and diced

Combine beef with 2 tablespoons of teriyaki sauce, and toss to coat. Set aside.

Cook noodles according to package directions.

While noodles cook, blend peanut butter, remaining teriyaki sauce, water, ginger, and hot pepper flakes in a medium bowl. When noodles are done, drain and add to bowl, tossing to coat with sauce. Keep warm.

Heat oil in a large nonstick skillet over medium-high heat. Add the beef and stir-fry until brown, approximately 2 minutes. Add to noodles and toss to coat. Sprinkle with diced cucumber and serve.

■ ■ ■

Seafood

Et Tuna, Brute?

SERVES 4

Surprisingly quick, this simple tuna and pasta dish can also be made with canned or cooked salmon. Serve it with a Caesar salad for maximum enjoyment, especially on the Ides of March.

½ lb. linguini, fettucine, or spaghetti

1 Tbs. olive oil

4 oz. mushrooms, sliced

1 medium onion, sliced

2 cups diced tomatoes

1 6½-oz. can tuna packed in water, drained and flaked

Pinch of hot red pepper flakes

1 Tbs. capers, rinsed and drained (optional)

6 large fresh basil leaves, minced

Freshly grated Parmesan or Romano cheese

Cook pasta in plenty of boiling water until done but still firm to the bite (al dente).

While pasta is cooking, heat the oil in a large nonstick skillet over medium heat. Add the mushrooms and onions, and sauté for 5 minutes. Add the tomatoes, tuna, pepper flakes, and capers. Bring to a boil, reduce heat, cover, and simmer for 5 minutes. Drain pasta and place in a serving bowl. Add the tuna mixture and basil, and toss well to combine. Serve with grated cheese on the side.

■ ■ ■

Tarragon Surimi   SERVES 4

Surimi is the "crabmeat look-alike" that's made from firm white fish and is considerably less expensive than crab. If you have crabmeat, however, don't hesitate to make this with the real thing. Be sure to serve with a fresh green salad on the side.

8 oz. shells, rotini, gemelli, or penne

1½ cups vegetable stock or fish stock, divided

6 large shallots, minced

½ tsp. dried tarragon or 1 tsp. chopped fresh tarragon

8 oz. surimi or crabmeat

1 cup evaporated skim milk or light cream

Salt and freshly ground black pepper, to taste

Paprika

Cook pasta in plenty of boiling water until done but still firm to the bite (al dente).

While the pasta cooks, heat ½ cup of the stock in a saucepan over medium heat. Add the shallots and tarragon, and cook for 5 minutes. Add the remaining stock, bring to a boil, and cook, uncovered, until volume is reduced to ½ cup. Add the surimi or crabmeat and evaporated milk or cream. Bring to a simmer and gently cook until surimi is heated through and sauce begins to thicken. Season to taste with salt and black pepper, and mix with drained pasta in a serving dish. Sprinkle with paprika and serve.

Orange-Salsa Salmon SERVES 4

Salmon, new potatoes, and fresh peas are the traditional Fourth of July feast in New England. Edible-pod sugar snap peas are a tasty variation on the traditional shell pea, and snow peas could be used as well. In this recipe, we add the flavors of the American Southwest and the Orient for a dish that is fit for a holiday or any day when you need something quick and easy.

3 Tbs. olive oil

1/4 cup orange juice

Freshly ground black pepper, to taste

4 salmon steaks, 4 to 6 oz. each

1 1/2 lbs. new red potatoes

1/2 lb. snap peas, stems and strings removed

1/2 cup salsa, mild or medium

1/3 cup orange marmalade

1 1/2 Tbs. tamari

1 Tbs. finely shredded fresh gingerroot

Combine oil, orange juice, and pepper. Brush both sides of salmon with mixture. Bake at 450°F (232°C), or grill, allowing about 10 minutes cooking time per inch of thickness measured at its thickest part, until salmon is cooked through and flakes when tested with a fork.

While salmon cooks, prepare potatoes and sauce. If potatoes are small, cook whole. Cut large potatoes in halves or quarters. Cook in boiling water for 10 to 15 minutes, until tender. Add snap peas to potatoes during last 5 minutes of cooking. Drain well.

In a small saucepan, combine salsa, marmalade, tamari, and ginger; mix well, bring to a boil, and remove from heat. Add two-thirds of sauce to potatoes and peas, and gently stir to coat.

Arrange salmon steaks on individual plates and spoon remaining sauce on top of each. Serve hot or chilled with potatoes and peas.

cold salads

vegetarian

Salad of the Americas

SERVES 6

Quinoa, corn, and beans—staple foods of the Incas, Mayas, and Aztecs—are combined with other foods native to the Americas—tomatoes and sunflower seeds—to produce a composed salad that is colorful, nutritious, and tasty.

1 cup quinoa, well-rinsed

1/2 cup cooked or frozen and thawed corn kernels

2 Tbs. lemon or lime juice, divided

3 scallions, minced

1 Tbs. olive oil

Salt and freshly ground black pepper, to taste

2 cups cooked black, pinto, or great northern beans, drained and rinsed if canned

1 large ripe tomato, peeled, seeded, and diced

1/4 cup chopped cilantro

1/4 cup unsalted sunflower seeds plus extra for garnish

In a medium saucepan, combine the quinoa and 2 cups of water; bring to a boil. Reduce the heat, cover, and simmer for 15 minutes or until all the liquid is absorbed. Fluff with a fork and allow to cool to room temperature.

Combine quinoa, corn, 1 tablespoon of the lemon juice, scallions, and oil in a bowl. Season to taste with salt and pepper.

In a separate bowl, combine the beans, tomato, remaining lemon juice, cilantro, and 1/4 cup sunflower seeds.

To serve, spread the bean mixture on a serving platter and mound the quinoa and corn on top. Garnish with additional sunflower seeds, if desired.

The Ultimate Greek Salad
SERVES 4

Mix together the flavors of Greece, and you have a deliciously cool summer salad. If you wish, add a can of drained and crumbled tuna to the vegetable mixture.

1 cup couscous, rice, or small pasta, uncooked

1 medium cucumber, seeded and diced

1 large ripe tomato, diced, with juice

1 red bell pepper, diced

1/2 medium red onion, thinly sliced

8 Kalamata olives, pitted and sliced

2 cups cooked garbanzo beans, rinsed and drained if canned

1/4 cup minced fresh Italian parsley

2 Tbs. extra-virgin olive oil

1 Tbs. lemon juice, or more to taste

1 garlic clove, minced or pressed

Salt and freshly ground black pepper, to taste

Romaine lettuce leaves, ripped to bite-size

2 oz. feta cheese, crumbled

Prepare couscous, rice, or small pasta as usual. Fluff couscous well; if using rice, be sure all liquid has been absorbed and rice is fairly dry, not sticky. If using pasta, rinse in cool water and drain well.

Toss together cucumber, tomato, pepper, onion, olives, garbanzos, and parsley. In a small bowl, mix together the olive oil, lemon juice, and garlic. Season to taste with salt and pepper, add to vegetables, and toss.

Arrange lettuce leaves on a platter. Mound the couscous, rice, or pasta on the lettuce. Cover with the mixed vegetables. Crumble the feta cheese over the top, and serve.

Southwestern Pasta Salad

SERVES 6

The flavors of the American Southwest combine with pasta to make a spicy, hearty summer salad full of beans, corn, peppers, and your favorite salsa in a low-fat creamy dressing. If you have time to make it ahead, this salad will benefit from a few hours in the refrigerator so the flavors can blend.

8 oz. medium shells, rotini, or other medium pasta

2 tsp. extra-virgin olive oil

1/2 tsp. ground cumin

2 cups cooked black beans, rinsed and drained if canned

2 cups cooked corn kernels

1 red bell pepper, cut into strips

6 scallions, thinly sliced

3/4 cup nonfat or low-fat mayonnaise

1/2 cup nonfat sour cream

1/3 cup hot, medium, or mild chunky salsa

2 Tbs. minced cilantro

Cook pasta in plenty of boiling water until done but still firm to the bite (al dente). Immediately drain and rinse with cold water. Toss with oil, sprinkle with cumin, and toss again. Add black beans, corn, pepper, and scallions.

Combine remaining ingredients in a small bowl. Add to salad, toss gently to mix, and serve.

Devilish Lentil Salad

SERVES 6

This salad is especially good when made ahead and allowed to cool thoroughly. Try it with the small French speckled green lentil, which takes a bit longer to cook but holds its shape better than the larger brown lentil. The ingredients in this recipe provide 54 percent of your daily fiber need.

1¼ cup French lentils

4⅔ cups water, divided

⅓ cup quinoa

1 large portabella mushroom, cubed

1 red bell pepper, chopped

2 cups diced tomato

3 scallions, sliced ¼-inch thick

¼ cup minced fresh Italian parsley

2 cloves garlic, minced

6 Tbs. extra-virgin olive oil

2 Tbs. red wine vinegar

1 Tbs. Dijon-style mustard

½ tsp. dried oregano or 1½ tsp. minced fresh oregano

⅛ tsp. cayenne pepper

Salt and freshly ground black pepper, to taste

Mixed salad greens

Check for stones, then rinse the lentils. Place in 4 cups of water and bring to a boil; cook 25 minutes. Lentils should still be somewhat firm.

While the lentils are cooking, rinse the quinoa well and bring to a boil in ⅔ cup of water; cover and simmer for 20 minutes.

In a large bowl, mix the mushroom, pepper, tomato, scallions, parsley, and garlic. Mix together the olive oil, vinegar, mustard, oregano, and cayenne pepper.

When the lentils and quinoa are done, drain well and add to the mixed vegetables. Pour dressing over the salad. Add salt and pepper to taste. Serve on a bed of fresh mixed salad greens.

Mediterranean Salad

SERVES 4

Bulgur is a fast-cooking form of wheat that is the mainstay of Middle East-ern salads, the most familiar being tabbouleh. This late-summer salad takes advantage of fresh cherry tomatoes and corn on the cob, but it can also be made any time of year with fresh or canned diced tomatoes and frozen corn that has been brought to room temperature.

1 cup vegetable stock	½ cup chopped cilantro
1 cup bulgur	¼ cup thinly sliced scallions
1 pint cherry tomatoes or 2 cups diced tomatoes	2 Tbs. chopped fresh mint
	3 Tbs. lime juice
1 cup cooked corn	1 Tbs. extra-virgin olive oil
1 cup diced cucumbers	2 cloves garlic, minced

Bring the stock to a boil in a 1-quart saucepan over high heat. Stir in the bulgur. Remove from the heat, cover, and let stand for 15 minutes, or until the bulgur is tender and the liquid has been absorbed. Fluff with a fork and transfer to a large bowl.

Halve the cherry tomatoes. Add the tomatoes, corn, cucumbers, cilantro, scallions, and mint to the bulgur. Toss the mixture lightly.

In a small bowl, whisk together the lime juice, oil, and garlic. Pour over the salad, and mix well.

■ ■ ■

chicken

Asian Chicken Salad

SERVES 4

This colorful salad combines small pasta shapes with poached chicken and a variety of vegetables that require no cooking. Make your own variations by adding cucumbers, snow pea pods, mushrooms, or other vegetables. Toast the almonds in a dry skillet or a 350°F (177°C) oven, stirring frequently, until golden brown.

½ lb. orzo, small shells, ditalini, or tiny bowties

½ lb. boneless, skinless chicken breast, cut into 1-inch cubes

4 oz. spinach leaves, stems discarded, sliced into strips

1 small red bell pepper, diced

1 cup fresh mung bean sprouts

2 scallions, sliced

3 Tbs. red or white wine vinegar

2 Tbs. tamari

1 Tbs. sesame oil

1 Tbs. prepared chili sauce or more to taste

1 Tbs. grated fresh gingerroot

¼ cup slivered almonds, toasted

Cook pasta in plenty of boiling water, until cooked but still firm (al dente). Drain, rinse with cold water, and drain well again.

While pasta is cooking, place chicken in a saucepan and cover with cold water. Bring to a boil, reduce the heat, and simmer until chicken is cooked through, about 5 minutes. Cut a piece open to be sure the chicken is no longer pink in the center. Drain and refrigerate cooked chicken until pasta is ready.

Combine chicken, pasta, spinach, pepper, sprouts, and scallions.

In a separate bowl, whisk together the remaining ingredients, except the almonds. Pour over the chicken mixture, mix well, and refrigerate until ready to serve. Sprinkle almonds over top just before serving.

Couscous Salad with Chicken SERVES 4

The chicken can be replaced with other cooked meats, or with grilled or sautéed portabella mushrooms.

5 Tbs. olive oil, divided

1/2 lb. boneless, skinless chicken breast, in 3/4-inch cubes

8 oz. broccoli florets, coarsely chopped

2 1/2 cups low-sodium, low-fat chicken stock, divided

1 large clove garlic, minced

1 1/2 tsp. dried marjoram or 1 Tbs. minced fresh marjoram

1 1/2 tsp. dried thyme or 1 1/2 Tbs. minced fresh thyme

3/4 cup uncooked couscous

2 Tbs. lemon juice

1/2 cup finely chopped fresh Italian parsley

2 drops hot pepper sauce

2 cups cooked garbanzo beans, rinsed and drained if canned

2 cups diced tomatoes

Heat 1 tablespoon oil in a large nonstick skillet over medium heat. Add the chicken, and sauté until opaque, about 5 minutes. Add broccoli florets and 1/2 cup chicken stock. Cover tightly and cook for 5 minutes more. Cut a piece open to be sure the chicken is no longer pink in the center. Cool mixture in its juices and refrigerate.

Bring 1 1/2 cups stock to a boil in a medium-sized saucepan. Add the garlic, marjoram, and thyme, and cook for 1 minute. Add the couscous, cover, and remove from the heat. Let stand for 5 minutes or until the liquid is absorbed. Fluff with a fork.

In a large bowl, mix the remaining 1/2 cup stock, oil, lemon juice, parsley, and hot pepper sauce. Add the couscous, and mix well. Let stand for 5 minutes. Add the garbanzos, tomatoes, chicken, broccoli, and pan juices, mix well, and serve.

Turkey

Granny Smith Summer Salad SERVES 4

Any small pasta can be used in this quick and cool summer salad that blends the flavor of smoked turkey with fat-free mayonnaise and yogurt and the crunch of apples and celery. Feel free to add or substitute your favorite summer vegetables—raw or lightly blanched—including crunchy edible-podded peas, carrots, radishes, or fennel. If you're a blue cheese fan, substitute blue for the feta cheese. Or try ricotta salata for a milder flavor. Pineapple or pears could replace or be added to the apple.

12 oz. ditalini, small shells, bowties, or elbow macaroni	1 medium Granny Smith apple, diced
¾ cup plain, nonfat yogurt	1 head leaf lettuce, leaves separated, washed, and drained
¼ cup fat-free mayonnaise	
12 oz. smoked turkey, sliced thick and diced	2 oz. crumbled feta cheese
2 celery stalks, diced	

Cook pasta in plenty of boiling water until done but still firm to the bite (al dente). Drain, rinse with cold water, and drain again.

Whisk together the yogurt and mayonnaise, and set aside.

In a large bowl, stir together the pasta, smoked turkey, celery, and apple. Add the sauce and toss until evenly coated. Arrange lettuce leaves on a serving dish and spoon the pasta onto the leaves. Sprinkle with cheese and serve.

San Antonio Summer Salad

SERVES 4

Make a cool summer salad out of the flavors of the Southwest using black beans, cumin, and your favorite spicy salsa. For a real summer taste, try a fresh salsa made from peak-of-the-season vegetables. Feel free to add or substitute your favorite ready-to-eat vegetables and greens in this quick and easy recipe. Serve with warm flour tortillas on the side.

4 cups packed, torn spinach leaves, stems discarded

1 red bell pepper, cut into short, thin strips

1 small red onion, sliced into thin rings

4 oz. mushrooms, sliced

2 cups cooked black beans, rinsed and drained if canned

8 oz. smoked turkey, sliced thick, cut into thin strips

1/2 cup fresh salsa, medium or hot

3 Tbs. canola oil

1 Tbs. cider or red wine vinegar

1/4 tsp. cumin

Combine vegetables, beans, and turkey in a large bowl. Mix salsa with oil, vinegar, and cumin in a small bowl. Pour over salad, toss lightly to coat, and chill until ready to eat. Toss again before serving.

Smoked Turkey and Rice Salad

SERVES 6

This recipe would also work well with leftover turkey or ham in place of the smoked turkey. When you have time, replace the brown rice with wild rice and add plumped dried cranberries. Substitute any crispy apple in season for the Granny Smiths. Toast the sliced almonds in a dry skillet or in a 350°F (177°C) oven for 5 to 10 minutes while the rice is cooking. Do not let the almonds burn.

6 servings instant brown rice, cooked according to package directions

8 oz. smoked turkey, sliced thick and diced

2 Granny Smith apples, diced

1 red bell pepper, diced

1 stalk celery, diced

2 Tbs. golden raisins

1/4 cup fresh lemon juice

1/3 cup apple juice or cider

2 Tbs. olive oil

2 Tbs. sliced almonds, toasted

Fluff cooked rice with a fork and place in a large bowl. Add the turkey, apples, peppers, celery, and raisins, and mix well. Whisk together the lemon juice, apple juice, and oil, and pour over the salad. Mix, sprinkle with toasted almonds, and serve.

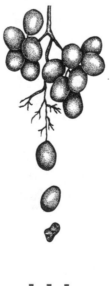

Cold Turkey Salad

SERVES 4

Roasted turkey from the deli makes this salad quick and easy. Use freshly harvested new potatoes, when available, and vary the other vegetables according to what is in season. The pecans add texture and flavor, but can be left out or replaced with walnuts, pine nuts, or sunflower seeds, if desired.

1 lb. small new potatoes, unpeeled

4 cups broccoli florets

1 medium red bell pepper, diced

1 celery stalk, chopped

1 medium carrot, peeled and chopped

8 oz. roasted turkey breast, sliced thick and cut into 3/4-inch cubes

1/2 cup chopped pecans (optional)

Spinach or leaf lettuce

DRESSING:

1/2 cup red or white wine vinegar or fresh lemon juice

2 Tbs. extra-virgin olive or canola oil

2 Tbs. prepared Dijon-style mustard

Freshly ground black pepper, to taste

Cut the potatoes into quarters and place in a large saucepan with water to cover. Bring to a boil, cover, reduce heat, and cook for 5 to 8 minutes or until potatoes are barely tender. Add the broccoli and cook for 2 minutes. Drain potatoes and broccoli well and transfer to a serving bowl. Add the bell pepper, celery, carrot, turkey, and pecans.

Whisk together the dressing ingredients in a small bowl and drizzle over the salad. Toss gently and serve on a bed of spinach or lettuce leaves.

Tuna

Tuscan Tuna Salad

SERVES 6

This light yet satisfying salad is bursting with Tuscany's favorite flavors—tuna and beans—plus it boasts the lively jalapeño "punch" of freshly made salsa and the goodness of pasta.

12 oz. small shells or elbows

2 6½-oz. cans white tuna packed in water

2 cups cooked cannellini or garbanzo beans, drained and rinsed if canned

½ cup pitted and sliced ripe olives

4 scallions, chopped

1 cup fresh salsa, mild or medium

1 Tbs. extra-virgin olive oil

2 Tbs. balsamic or red wine vinegar

1 tsp. dried basil or 1 Tbs. minced fresh basil

3 cups shredded spinach leaves, stems discarded

Cook pasta in plenty of boiling water until done but still firm to the bite (al dente). Drain and rinse in cold water to cool.

While pasta is cooking, drain tuna and break into chunks. Combine tuna, beans, olives, and scallions in a large bowl. Mix salsa with oil, vinegar, and basil in a small bowl, and add to the tuna mixture. Toss lightly. Add cooked pasta, and mix gently. Arrange spinach on a serving plate, top with tuna and pasta mixture, and serve.

Lemon Linguine with Tuna

SERVES 6

Combine hot linguine with a lemon dressing to infuse the pasta with flavor, then mix with tuna, peas, and tomatoes for a light summer dish that can be served at room temperature or chilled. Fresh tuna, lightly grilled, makes a wonderful summer substitution for canned, as do fresh peas in season.

12 oz. linguine

1/2 cup fresh lemon juice

1/4 cup extra-virgin olive oil

4 scallions, sliced thin

2 tsp. dried Italian herb mix, or 1 tsp. dried basil, 1/2 tsp. dried oregano, 1/4 tsp. dried thyme, and 1/4 tsp. crushed dried rosemary or 1 Tbs. minced fresh basil, 1 1/2 tsp.

minced fresh oregano, 3/4 tsp. fresh thyme, and 3/4 tsp. minced fresh rosemary

Salt and freshly ground black pepper, to taste

2 6 1/2-oz. cans tuna packed in water, drained and flaked

2 cups lightly blanched peas or frozen peas, thawed

2 cups diced tomato

Cook pasta in plenty of boiling water until done but still firm to the bite (al dente).

In a large bowl, whisk together lemon juice, oil, scallions, herbs, salt, and pepper. Add hot linguine and toss. Add tuna and peas, and mix well. Chill until ready to serve. Add tomatoes, and toss just before serving.

Insalata Rossa

When you have time, roast your own red peppers beside the tomatoes, but for a quick and easy meal, take advantage of jarred roasted peppers. Capers add a spicy punch, and you can easily add cucumbers, celery, or other raw vegetables to this salad lightly dressed with olive oil and lemon juice.

2 cups low-sodium chicken or
vegetable stock

1¼ cup couscous or 1 cup long-
grain white rice

2 medium tomatoes

2 large red peppers, roasted and
cut into strips

1 6½-ounce can tuna packed in
water, drained and flaked

2 Tbs. capers, rinsed and drained

2 Tbs. extra-virgin olive oil

3 Tbs. fresh lemon juice

Salt and freshly ground black
pepper, to taste

Bring the stock to a boil. If using couscous, add the couscous, remove from the heat, cover, and let sit for 5 minutes or until liquid is absorbed. Fluff with a fork. Set aside. If using rice, add the rice, return to a boil, cover, and simmer for 20 minutes or until rice is cooked and stock is absorbed. Fluff with a fork and set aside.

Preheat broiler. Place tomatoes on a baking sheet. Broil tomatoes until skins begin to split and blacken in spots, about 4 minutes, turning occasionally. Cool. Peel tomatoes. Cut into wedges. Gently combine tomatoes, peppers, tuna, and capers.

Whisk together oil and lemon juice in a small bowl. Season to taste with salt and pepper. Drizzle over salad and serve with couscous or rice on the side.

Index

■ ■ ■

CHELSEA GREEN

Sustainable living has many facets. Chelsea Green's celebration of the sustainable arts has led us to publish trend-setting books about organic gardening, solar electricity and renewable energy, innovative building techniques, regenerative forestry, local and bioregional democracy, and whole foods. The company's published works, while intensely practical, are also entertaining and inspirational, demonstrating that an ecological approach to life is consistent with producing beautiful, eloquent, and useful books, videos, and audio cassettes.

For more information about Chelsea Green, or to request a free catalog, call toll-free (800) 639-4099, or write to us at P.O. Box 428, White River Junction, Vermont 05001. Visit our Web site at www.chelseagreen.com.

Chelsea Green's titles include:

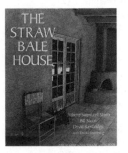 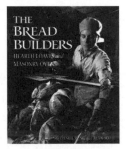 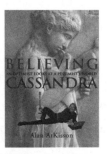

The Straw Bale House
The New Independent Home
Independent Builder:
   Designing & Building a
   House Your Own Way
The Rammed Earth House
The Passive Solar House
The Earth-Sheltered House
The Sauna
Wind Energy Basics
The Solar Living Sourcebook
A Shelter Sketchbook
Mortgage-Free!
Hammer. Nail. Wood.
Stone Circles

The Bread Builders
Whole Foods Companion
Simple Food for the
   Good Life
The Apple Grower
The Flower Farmer
Passport to Gardening
The New Organic Grower
Four-Season Harvest
Solar Gardening
Straight-Ahead Organic
The Contrary Farmer
The Contrary Farmer's
   Invitation to Gardening
Good Spirits

Believing Cassandra
Gaviotas: A Village to
   Reinvent the World
Loving and Leaving the
   Good Life
Scott Nearing: The Making
   of a Homesteader
Who Owns the Sun?
Global Spin:
   The Corporate Assault
   on Environmentalism
Beyond the Limits
The Man Who Planted Trees
The Northern Forest
Seeing Nature